By Forrest B. Marchington and Ethan Skemp

Credits

Authors: Forrest B. Marchinton & Ethan Skemp
Second Edition Authors: Andrew Bates, Phil Brucato, Lon Franson, Devin Parker
Developer: Ethan Skemp
Editor: Aileen E. Miles
Art: Mitch Byrd, Brian LeBlanc
Screen Art: Steve Prescott & Sherilyn Van Valkenburgh
Cover Art: Joe Corroney
Cover Design, Layout & Typesetting: Aileen E. Miles

Shame-Faced Apology

Our deepest apologies to Chris Howard, who was mistakenly excluded from the credits of **A World of Rage**, due to our own stupid bone-headedness. The slight wasn't intentional, Chris. We'd be happy to crawl out from under our desks and apologize in person if you could see fit to call off your ex-KGB pals now.

735 PARK NORTH BLVD.
SUITE 128
CLARKSTON, GA 30021
USA

For a free White Wolf catalog call 1-800-454-WOLF.

Check out White Wolf online at

http://www.white-wolf.com; alt.games.whitewolf and rec.games.frp.storyteller

PRINTED IN THE USA.

Contents

The Tribes

As already stated, the Thirteenth Tribe has withdrawn from the Garou Nation for personal reasons. This act of separatism has created a great rift between them and the other tribes. Even the Stargazers who remain with their old allies fall under a cloud of suspicion. They are still Garou — but to most eyes, no longer fighting quite the same war as their cousins.

You may allow players to generate Stargazer characters if you so choose. However, be warned: Some players will do so in an attempt to be "different," in hopes of drawing more attention to themselves. If you allow non-standard characters of this sort, you have an obligation to make certain that these individuals receive no more than their fair share of your attention. **Werewolf** is at heart a game about the Garou Nation, and it's a bad idea to penalize players who want to play full-fledged members of the Nation by favoring players who would rather do something else.

Stargazers

The Stargazers have always been outsiders to the rest of the Garou Nation. Unlike other werewolves, they seemed content to remain aloof and solitary, joining packs but never seeming to crave companionship. They possessed no lands of their own, at least within the Garou Nation's typical borders. They were able to wield serenity as a weapon, and were more successful in mastering their Rage than any other tribe had ever been. Their awareness of body, mind and spirit gave them a graceful unity, one that they expressed both through their mastery of riddles and through their specialized martial art, Kailindo. They were few in number, strange loners who served as strong allies, if rarely as bosom friends.

Despite all this, it came as a great shock to the other tribes when the Stargazers announced their intention to withdraw from the Garou Nation for an unspecified period of time. Only a few saw such a move coming — a rare few that had carefully watched the Stargazers slowly wither from lack of focus.

It would seem that the Stargazers' troubles stemmed in no small part from their philosophy. In order to throw off the Weaver's strands, Stargazers trained themselves to forgo attachments to material things, resources, even other people. The tribe's numbers shrank as their enlightenment grew; breeding was something of an afterthought to the Stargazers, and holding territory seemed to be as much a burden as anything else. Unfortunately, this made the tribe all the more vulnerable when the small territory they *did* possess came under attack.

In the latter part of the 20th century, the forces of the Wyrm captured multiple Stargazer caerns in their ancestral home in the Himalayas and India. The Stargazers were appalled by this, but found themselves lacking the numbers to properly retaliate. When the tribal elders requested help from their fellow tribes, the answer they received was heartbreaking. The Garou Nation's lands simply didn't extend into Asia; the Stargazers' lands were just on the fringe of what the Nation called its own. Worse, the Garou no longer had the numbers to spare for such an effort — to send their own warriors deep into hostile territory would leave too many caerns understaffed and vulnerable to attack. With the Black Spiral Dancers known to be strong throughout the Garou Nation's territory, it was just too much of a risk. Though it pained many elders of all tribes to admit it, they were in no position to help. If the Stargazers were to retake their ancestral lands, they would need assistance from another source.

Surprisingly, in early 2000, the Stargazers received it.

Several of the tribe's elders had long been in contact with the shapeshifters of Asia, who were organized into a society not unlike the Garou Nation. This coalition of Eastern shapeshifters, the Beast Courts of the Emerald Mother, had long been pursuing an extended alliance with the Stargazers. Finally, in late 1999, the Courts sent emissaries to the Stargazers' most senior elders, bearing a simple message:

"It grieves us deeply to hear of the loss of Shigalu Monastery, long hailed as a pearl of wisdom set in the brow of the Himalayas. We offer our condolences to the esteemed tribe known as the Stargazers, and propose this: If the Stargazers are willing to enter into alliance with our own poor courts, we would be honored to provide our cousins with war parties and intelligence to assist them in their struggle to retake their lands."

After long debate, the Stargazers reached a decision. They sent a message of simple acceptance and thanks to the Beast Courts — and then they began to explain their decision to the rest of the Garou Nation. Although the news wasn't taken very well, the Nation agreed that it was better to let the Stargazers withdraw peacefully than to ignite another bloody civil war in the name of "unity." And so the Stargazers began to leave.

Of course, not all Stargazers agree with this philosophy. Many, particularly the younger ones, think of themselves as Westerners first and foremost, and proud members of the Garou Nation to boot. These dissidents wound up striking a compromise with their elders. As agreed, they will remain where they like for a time, and assist their allies among the other tribes. In return, they will send any new-Changed Stargazer cubs to their elders to be trained with the bulk of the tribe, and they will respond to the call of their elders if the need is there.

Life isn't easy for the Stargazers who remain with a foot in each world. Most of their tribe gently disapproves of their independence, whereas the rest of the Garou Nation tends to look at them suspiciously, as if they might desert a fight at any moment to rejoin their relatives. But nobody ever said that being Garou was easy, and these Stargazers have decided that honor requires them to follow their consciences, no matter the obstacles.

Appearance: The Stargazers are a truly multiethnic tribe; they have adopted the children of many bloodlines into their own. Many are European, African or Middle to Near Eastern in ancestry; however, most Pure Bred Stargazers reflect the tribe's original territory in the Himalayas, India and the Far East. Their coats run the gamut from pale gray to deep black, and a light striped pattern isn't uncommon. They tend toward lean and athletic build rather than thick musculature, and most carry themselves with a quiet calm.

Kinfolk: The Stargazer tribe is sadly lacking in strong Kin support; their tendency to preach self-discipline and limited attachments to humans or wolves cuts down on the number of casual conceptions. The tribe originally bred with the people of India and the Himalayas, but as the Stargazers spread across the globe, they adopted many ethnicities as Kin. The tribe is particularly interested in keeping their wolf blood and instincts strong, and so the Stargazers are inclined to seek out wolf mates more frequently than one might expect. Their human Kin tend to be intellectuals, and are often people of strong convictions besides. Most aren't particularly rich or influential, but they usually have a variety of skills that their relatives may call upon.

Territory: The Stargazers have precious little territory left to call their own. Many of their ancient caerns in the Himalayas have fallen to Wyrmish forces that have used China's military maneuvers as cover. What's more, the tribe was unwilling to forcibly take caerns from the other tribes, and as a result has very few caerns of their own in the Americas or Europe. This lack of definitive "Stargazer territory" has made the decision to withdraw easier for the tribal elders, who are currently seeking the means to retake some of the tribe's ancestral lands from the Wyrm.

Tribal Totem: Chimera

Initial Willpower: 4

Background Restrictions: When a cub is adopted into the Stargazers, the first thing his teachers instruct him to do is to rely on himself first and foremost. Part of this learning process involves severing oneself from material things that one might rely on; Stargazer characters may not begin play with Resources or Fetish. What's more, the Stargazers have, for the most part, burned their bridges with the Garou Nation; a Stargazer may not take any Allies among the Garou Nation or their friends without explicit Storyteller permission.

Beginning Gifts: Balance, Falling Touch, Sense Wyrm

Quote: *In the quest to spread our branches, we have lost our roots. Forgive us, cousins, but we must set ourselves right before we can be of any use to others.*

Stereotypes

Solemn Voice, a Stargazer Philodox, remembers his old cohorts:

Black Furies: We are all destined to be incarnated as male and female alike in turn; how much can the Furies know if they refuse to learn from half their lifetimes?

Bone Gnawers: They are braver than anyone thinks. They guard the doors that nobody else will guard.

Children of Gaia: We are much alike. If they chose to pursue their goals apart from the Garou Nation as we did, we would welcome their company.

Fianna: They are very much in love with their own bodies and the joy of being alive. They were always stronger in numbers, if weaker in discipline.

Get of Fenris: Strong of body, strong of spirit, weak in compassion. If only they realized they were one-third flawed.

Glass Walkers: The very fact that the Glass Walkers hold so much influence in the Garou Nation is a sign that we were right to leave. We cannot effectively sever the strands of the Weaver in a place where werewolves gladly anchor her lines.

Red Talons: I respect the purity of their instinct, from which wisdom flows, and mourn their attachment to their hatred — and I desperately hope that the one is not equal to the other.

Shadow Lords: They value cunning and call it wisdom. They are one of the strongest reasons why we cannot rely on others to understand our needs any longer.

Silent Striders: They will always be welcome in our lands. If anyone understands why we must follow our own path, they do.

Silver Fangs: Even if there is reason for such pride, it is still a fault to let it consume you.

Uktena: They are a cautionary parable. In contemplating the nature of your enemy, there is always the danger of opening doors in your heart through which it may enter.

Wendigo: We parted without ever really becoming friends. It is a humbling loss.

Tribal Weaknesses (Optional)

Storytellers looking to throw an additional bit of spice into their players' lives may be interested in the idea of tribal weaknesses. These are inborn flaws of character that each member of a tribe possesses — if you choose to use this rule, of course. The main advantage to this rule is that it makes membership in a tribe more of a double-edged sword, emphasizing that as far as family is concerned, you take the bad with the good. However, you should be fair about using these weaknesses; if you decide to use these rules, be sure to let the players know, so they don't feel that you're persecuting them.

Some tribal weaknesses are social in nature; others may be genetic, or even imposed by the tribe's spirit nature or connection to their totem. It's the Storyteller's responsibility to enforce each weakness; the players might conveniently "forget" now and again to play up their handicaps when the relevant situation arises.

Of course, you don't always have to enforce a tribal weakness, even if you've chosen to use these optional rules. Many weaknesses can be overcome, or might not apply in given situations. Of course, these exemptions should be relatively rare (or otherwise a tribal weakness isn't really a weakness at all), but they help make a weakness seem more like the flaws of character that they are and less like laws of nature.

Black Furies

Anger: -1 difficulty to enter frenzy when provoked by men

The Black Furies have no tolerance for abusive men; they have seen first-hand the sort of violence a man is capable of visiting on a woman or child, and they bear those memories within them. Pegasus herself reinforces the Furies' refusal to accept domineering males as "part of the natural order." Whenever a Fury must make a frenzy check brought on by a male human (or werecreature, or vampire, or similar sentient humanlike being), her difficulty is reduced by 1, to a minimum of 2. This weakness might be overcome in cases where the Fury is dealing with a man she has otherwise learned to trust implicitly, or a man she cares for deeply.

Bone Gnawers

Social Outcasts: +1 difficulty on all Social rolls involving other tribes

The rest of the Garou Nation just doesn't have much respect for the Bone Gnawers. Even when a

Gnawer achieves a remarkable feat, the praise often bears the unpleasant tone of "He did very well indeed...particularly for one of his tribe." As a result, Bone Gnawers generally suffer a +1 difficulty modifier to any Social rolls made to impress, intimidate or otherwise deal with other tribes. This weakness is generally overcome on a case-by-case basis, as other werewolves learn to respect and even admire the Bone Gnawer in question.

Children of Gaia

Weak Veil: Witnesses at +4 on Delirium Chart

Because the Children of Gaia did not participate fervently in the Impergium, their tribal totem has granted them an extra measure of serenity. Humans who see a Child of Gaia in Crinos form do not suffer from the Delirium as strongly, and their reaction on the Delirium chart is shifted up four places (to "Terror" at the worst). Some Children of Gaia do not see this as a weakness, but the reality is that without the added protection of the Veil, the Children are in danger of violating one of the Litany's most sacred laws. There is no reliable way to undo this flaw; in fact, if the Child of Gaia begins causing strong Delirium reactions again, it's likely to be at random (and unhelpful) intervals.

Fianna

Low Self-Control: All Willpower rolls are at +1 difficulty

The Fianna are a headily emotional tribe, given to bursts of manic joy, flashes of murderous anger and bouts of severe melancholia. Their philosophy is to live life to its fullest — a philosophy that, sadly, does not promote quite as much discipline as would be preferable.

Get of Fenris

Intolerance

No Get of Fenris is ever encouraged to compromise her ideals. The tribe's constant emphasis on fighting a never-ending battle and showing no weakness tends to breed a rather intolerant point of view. Every Get has a particular object of contempt, something she cannot abide. When confronted with this stimulus, she will be unable to endure its presence and will do everything in her power to rid herself of the annoyance.

The player may either define a specific Intolerance for her character (with the Storyteller's approval) or choose from the list below. Wyrm creatures may *not* be chosen — all Garou, particularly Fenrir, are expected to be intolerant of the Wyrm.

• **Cowardice** — You hate cowardice in all its forms, whether fear of bloodshed or fear of taking charge in social situations. Anyone in your pack who demonstrates cowardice must answer to you. If the tables are turned, and *you* go into a fox frenzy, you are so consumed with self-loathing that you take unnecessary risks trying to atone for your moment of weakness.

• **Compromise** — You see compromise as no better than outright capitulation. To compromise is to surrender, and you scorn those who advocate such tactics. You refuse to compromise any of your beliefs of your own accord; if a leader forces you to do so, that is fair, but it does not speak well for the leader's judgement.

• **Lower Animals** — Respect Those Beneath Ye? Hardly! As far as you are concerned, that's a poor Litany rule. You defend creatures lower than you as is your duty, but such wretches — including humans and wolves — deserve not a whit of respect. A grave insult from a human is enough to drive you toward frenzy.

• **Weakness** — You hate physical or moral weakness in others, scorning those you deem weak and refusing to tolerate such qualities in yourself. This leads you to be quite unmerciful — those who need sparing, in your mind, don't deserve it.

• **Weaver Stuff** — You're convinced that the Weaver is the grand enemy, and refuse to let too much of her stuff near you — especially technology. You especially despise the Glass Walkers and all urrah. Weapons more complicated than bows or swords are of no interest to you; the same goes for other technological items, *particularly* luxury items.

Glass Walkers

Weaver Affinity: Cannot regain Gnosis in wilderness

The Glass Walkers' unique affinity to the spiritual patterns of the cities limits them when they are away from their chosen environment. They have difficulty drawing on the Wyld's energies away from urban regions, and cannot regain Gnosis in the wilds (save when at a caern).

Red Talons

Wyld Affinity: Cannot regain Gnosis in cities

Conversely, the Red Talons' close ties to the spiritual texture of the wilderness impair them when they leave its embrace. Talons may not regain Gnosis within a city, save when within an actual caern.

Shadow Lords

Failure's Dagger: -1 Renown for failure

Shadow Lords do not tolerate failure. Whenever a Shadow Lord fails to carry out a task that would normally gain him Glory, Honor or Wisdom, he instead loses one point of temporary Renown in that category. (If he would have gained Renown in more than one category, subtract only from the category that would have been awarded the most.) This is in addition to any Renown normally lost for his actions. This does not affect the normal Renown process in any other way; if the Shadow Lord succeeds in the action, then he gains the normal amount of Renown.

Silent Striders

Haunted

The Silent Striders bear a twofold curse: they can no longer rest within the boundaries of their ancestral homeland, and they are haunted by the spirits of the dead. When a Strider botches the roll to step sideways, she sends ripples through the Dark Umbra, alerting any nearby wraiths or walking dead to her presence. It's almost certain that *something* will show up to either demand the Strider's aid or try to destroy her; in areas like old battlegrounds, cemeteries or similar places of the dead, the Strider may attract far too much attention for her own good.

Note: The Silent Strider fifth level Gift: Reach the Umbra will allow a Strider to enter and exit the Umbra without fear of this curse.

Silver Fangs

Derangement

Years of inbreeding with limited flocks of Kinfolk have taken their toll on the Silver Fangs. Each Silver Fang begins play with a Derangement that can be overcome only temporarily. The character's madness may be chosen by the player (with the Storyteller's approval) or taken from the list below.

• **Amnesia** — In a highly stressful and traumatic situation, you forget who you are.

• **Manic-Depression** — You suffer from wild mood swings ranging from wild bliss to utter despair. You begin each story in one phase or the other and can switch back and forth for any number of reasons.

• **Multiple Personalities** — There are a number of different personalities housed within your head. You may switch your name, Nature and Demeanor during times of great stress.

• **Obsession** — You tend to latch on to someone or something and make him or it the focal point of your life.

• **Paranoia** — You see the Wyrm's influence in everything. Don't the others see it too? Perhaps they've been corrupted as well.

• **Perfection** — You work hard to keep everything in your life going perfectly at all times. You use all of your energy to prevent things from going wrong and have been known to frenzy when things don't go in your favor.

• **Power Madness** — You are obsessed with control and dominance over others.

• **Regression** — You tend to revert to childlike (or cublike) behavior during times of extreme stress.

Stargazers

Obsessive Mind Games

The Stargazer who fails an Enigmas roll becomes obsessed with the riddle, unable to concentrate on anything else until he finds the solution. During this time, the Storyteller may choose from a number of minor effects to represent this inward obsession (only one at a time, though). Examples include shutting the world out (+1 difficulty to all Perception rolls) or a slow reaction to outside stimuli (+1 difficulty to all Initiative rolls).

Uktena

Intense Curiosity

The Uktena are almost pathologically compelled to unravel any mysteries presented to them; their totem is a spirit of secrets and hidden lore, and they feel a very strong compulsion to bring more knowledge to Uktena's side. When an Uktena learns that somebody knows something he doesn't, he becomes distracted until he's able to wrest the secret free. The Storyteller may impose various penalties on the character until he can learn the secret. Examples include having trouble concentrating (+1 difficulty for all Willpower rolls), a short temper (-1 difficulty to frenzy) or a surly disposition (+1 difficulty for Social rolls).

However, when an Uktena has gained the truth behind a secret in a particularly ingenious or clever fashion, he may gain a temporary point of Wisdom Renown or regain a point of spent Willpower (Storyteller's option).

Wendigo

Wheel of the Seasons

The Wendigo have long lived in a very close relationship with the Earth and its ever-changing seasons. They have a different weakness during different times of the year, but they gain power in winter, the season of their totem.

Spring: +1 difficulty to Willpower rolls; the vibrancy of new life distracts the Wendigo.

Summer: -1 difficulty to frenzy rolls; summer is the traditional season of war.

Fall: +1 difficulty to change forms; the world slows down in autumn, and fewer new things are born.

Winter: -1 difficulty on soak rolls; winter is the Wendigo's season, and they use their hate and anger to fortify themselves during this time.

The Fera

In the War of Rage, the Garou decimated the other breeds of shapeshifters that populated the world. Many races were driven to extinction. Others were whittled down to a fraction of their numbers, and driven into hiding. The werewolves have heard little or nothing of them ever since. However, a few of these other shapeshifters — the Fera — still survive.

Needless to say, few of the Fera count the Garou as allies. Most are raised on tales of the werewolves murdering their ancestors, and are taught never to so much as show themselves to a Garou. However, sometimes curiosity gets the better of a young shapeshifter. Sometimes a Fera who still feels loyalty to Gaia crosses paths with a werewolf pack when chasing the same Wyrmish prey. And sometimes a Fera deliberately seeks out a werewolf in the name of revenge. Such encounters aren't common — but they do happen.

There have never been any shapeshifters born of domestic animals; the spark of Gnosis is apparently too dim in domesticated breeds to birth werecreatures. For example, legend holds that there was once a race of "bull-shifters," shapeshifters who bred with the mighty aurochs, a powerful breed of wild cattle — but these Fera were unable to carry on their line with domestic cattle (and only desperation would have forced them to even try). When the aurochs died out, all hope of a reborn race of bull-shifters died with them.

There isn't room in this book to detail the Fera, Traits and all, as thoroughly as we might like. Each Changing Breed is detailed separately in their own Changing Breed book, from **Bastet** and **Nuwisha** to **Rokea** and **Nagah** (the latter two available in 2001). The following summaries, however, should offer beginning Storytellers a brief overview on the sorts of creatures sharing Gaia's blessing, and even experienced Storytellers may find the sample shapeshifter statistics helpful in a pinch. Each entry comes with an overview of "Suggested Traits" that the Storyteller may find useful in building Fera antagonists or rivals, and a sample member of the Breed in question (with Attributes in parentheses representing the Crinos form, or similar war form if no Crinos exists). Gift lists given are also very vague; Storytellers should feel free to add extra Gifts to Fera if they seem particularly appropriate (such as a wereraven possessing a Gift that is taught by a raven-spirit), even at lower levels than the Garou might learn them. (Conversely, Gifts taught by wolf-spirits should be of a higher level for Fera than they are for Garou...)

Ananasi

Perhaps the most alien and disturbing of shapeshifters are the Ananasi, the werespiders. Even the Rokea, cold-blooded though they may be, don't breed with invertebrates. The Ananasi are a mysterious and ruthless race, driven by intricate laws to pursue their own ends. They remain largely aloof from the battle for Gaia, instead working for the direct benefit of their race — and possibly toward some other, more ambitious goal.

The werespiders rarely act in large numbers; like most Fera, they aren't really pack creatures. There might be three or four werespiders in any city of significant size and importance (about the size of Raleigh or Cannes) — more in larger cities, where they have more room to hide. The Ananasi of any given area keep in loose contact with one another, cooperating when the need is there and acting alone the rest of the time.

It's very rare for a werewolf to cross paths with an Ananasi and actually know it; the werespiders prefer to keep out of sight for reasons of survival, and their notably unemotional nature doesn't drive them to seek revenge for age-old vendettas. Even so, a Garou pack — particularly one that travels in Glass Walker circles — might accidentally stumble into a werespider's web of intrigue. What happens next is entirely up to the pack and the werespider in question....

Suggested Traits: The Ananasi do not possess Rage; instead, they must drink fresh mammalian blood to fuel their powers. An Ananasi has a blood pool of up to ten "blood points" (although higher-rank werespiders may possess more). The werespider may spend a blood point to heal a health level of non-aggravated damage, to gain an extra action in a turn, or to generate webbing (which is as strong as one might expect). When she runs out of blood points, she's very hungry, but suffers no other ill effects. Ananasi can gain nutrition from the blood of other shapeshifters — and some enjoy the taste of such a "treat" — but cannot drink the blood of the undead.

Without Rage, the werespiders are not especially vulnerable to silver. They can enter the Penumbra without rites or Gifts, but find it easier to do where the Gauntlet is high and much more difficult in areas without many strands of the Weaver's webs. They have multiple limbs in some forms, but do not gain any extra actions from this benefit any more than a person with two hands can perform a separate complicated action with each hand. (They do find grappling easier with multiple limbs, however.)

Generally speaking, each Ananasi tends to follow one of the Triat rather than Gaia. This choice affects their supernatural abilities. The Weaver's followers (the most numerous) tend to have Gifts and rites like those of the Glass Walkers, the Wyld-aspected werespiders have Black Fury and Uktena-like traits, and the Wyrmish Ananasi use tricks like those of the Black Spiral Dancers.

The Ananasi can take four forms — a human form, a twisted human/spider hybrid (which varies from werespider to werespider), a spider the size of a Volkswagen and a giant swarm of normal-sized spiders. When in the swarm form, the Ananasi can be hurt and even killed, but only by destroying every last spider (who can all flee in separate directions). An Ananasi who loses most of her spiders in this form, or whose component spiders scatter too far from one another, can still reform in full health over time, although she's likely to lose anywhere from 50-90% of her memories. In this way, the Ananasi can survive many perils — but always at a cost.

Corporate Puppeteer

Attributes: Strength 2 (6), Dexterity 3 (5), Stamina 2 (5), Charisma 2, Manipulation 4 (1), Appearance 4 (0), Intelligence 3, Perception 3, Wits 2

[**Note:** The Attributes in parentheses don't represent a Crinos form, but rather the Ananasi's "Pithus" form — a hideous spider the size of a compact car. Although her Pithus (or "Pit Spider") form weighs only 160 pounds or so, it's strong and durable well beyond its bulk.]

Abilities: Alertness 2, Dodge 1, Empathy 1, Intimidation 2, Primal-Urge 1, Subterfuge (casual conversation) 4, Drive 2, Etiquette 3, Firearms 2, Performance 2, Stealth 3, Computer 3, Enigmas 1, Investigation 4 (blackmail), Law 2, Linguistics 2, Politics 3, Rituals 3, Science 1

Gifts: (1) Control Simple Machine, Open Seal, Persuasion, Resist Toxin; (2) Jam Technology, Power Surge, Sense of the Prey, Taking the Forgotten [can apply to blood drained from a victim]; (3) Reshape Object, Venom Blood, Visceral Agony; (4) Cocoon

Blood pool: 12; **Gnosis:** 4; **Willpower:** 7

Attacks: Bite (7 dice), claw (7 dice). The Ananasi's venom automatically and instantly paralyzes mortals. By spending a Gnosis point, she can paralyze supernatural creatures such as werewolves and even vampires; to do so, she must roll Gnosis against a difficulty of the victim's Stamina + 4 (maximum 9). To recover from this paralysis, the victim must do the equivalent of healing four levels of lethal damage; for example, a paralyzed Garou would have to regenerate for four turns (without actually healing any wounds he might have) until the poison is neutralized.

Roleplaying Hints: As a creature of the Weaver, the Corporate Puppeteer is equally at home in boardrooms or sewer tunnels. Without the threat of Rage driving her to frenzy, she is able to live a double life; her day job is the personal assistant to one of the most prominent corporate figures in the city. With access to his contact list and secrets alike, she is able to push forward her own agendas with remarkable subtlety. At night, she frequents the most exclusive, trendiest nightclubs — where she finds her prey. She is rumored to have a few connections — or even pawns — among the vampire community, although this may simply be paranoia. She avoids combat, preferring to attack enemies through third parties or by stealth, but if pressed reverts to the form of a monstrous black widow and strikes to kill.

Bastet

The Bastet are some of the Garou's bitterest rivals, and in many ways the polar opposites of the werewolves. The Bastet are werecats — not shapeshifters who take the form of domestic cats, but rather werebeasts whose animal forms are those of the great cats of the world. Where werewolves are pack animals, werecats are loners. The Garou are social and feel ill-at-ease working without others of their kind; the Bastet hoard their secrets, reluctant to trust others. The bad blood between Bastet and Garou is legendary; even life-and-death situations are no sure way to convince the two races to cooperate.

Although very few Garou could name them all, there are nine tribes of Bastet in existence.

• The **Bagheera** are the wereleopards of Africa and Asia, and serve as lorekeepers to their kind. They are the tribe most likely to deal with other Bastet tribes, although they are still loners at heart.

• The **Balam** are the werejaguars of Central and South America, an embittered and decimated tribe of warriors desperately trying to hold on to what's left of their territory.

• The **Bubasti**, sorcerous werecats with ties to ancient Egypt, are on the brink of extinction. Their Kyphur cat Kin are apparently extinct, and other Bastet tribes whisper that the Bubasti have made some sort of "deal with the devil" to survive as long as they have without feline breeding stock.

• Only a very few **Ceilican**, the fey and witch-touched European wildcat-shifters, survive in the 21st century. The tribe underwent three great purges — the first being the War of Rage, the second a feud with the fae during the Middle Ages, and the most recent an attack by the Black Spiral Dancers on their greatest conclave. Those that survive have gone back into hiding, perhaps never to reemerge.

• The **Khan** weretigers are the warrior nobility of the Bastet, powerful lords with as strong a sense of honor as is to be found among the cat-shifters. Regrettably, the waning fortunes of the tiger species have put the Khan in similar straits; like the Ceilican and Bubasti, they may soon die out forever.

• The werecougar **Pumonca** are survivors first, loners second, and servants of Gaia third. After suffering heavy losses in the Second War of Rage, they retreated to the mountains, where they jealously guard their secluded territories even today.

• The **Qualmi** werelynxes are a particularly secretive lot, given to hiding in the farthest northwoods and speaking solely in riddles. These creatures have much in common with the Uktena; a few very secret alliances between the two are quite possible.

• The **Simba** are the werelions, and they are every inch as proud and belligerent as one might expect. They are one of only two Bastet tribes to actively cooperate in prides, and a Simba pride is every inch as dangerous as a Garou pack.

• The other cooperative tribe, the **Swara** werecheetahs are a particularly reclusive breed, very much concerned with the preservation of their families and cheetah Kin. They are swift as the wind, possibly with the potential to be even greater messengers than the Silent Striders.

Suggested Traits: Bastet are not as strong as Garou, although they are quicker and more dexterous. They are equally likely to specialize in Physical, Social or Mental Attributes; the werecats enjoy physical prowess, seduction and mental challenges in equal portions. Gifts of perception, stealth and sheer dexterity summarize the Bastet focus best, although individual Bastet are fond of mystical tricks, and might possess a "surprising" Gift or two. The werecats' greatest weakness is that they cannot step sideways as easily as most Garou do; this requires the use of a Level Four Gift, although some werecats are able to circumvent the Gauntlet within an area they've ritually marked as their own.

Bagheera Spy

Attributes: Strength 2 (5), Dexterity 4 (6), Stamina 3 (5), Charisma 3, Manipulation 3 (0), Appearance 3 (0), Intelligence 3, Perception 3, Wits 3

Abilities: Alertness 4, Athletics 2, Brawl 2, Dodge 3, Intimidation 1, Primal-Urge 2, Streetwise 2, Subterfuge 3, Drive 1, Etiquette 2, Melee 1, Performance 2, Stealth 4, Survival 2, Enigmas 2, Investigation 3, Linguistics 1, Occult 1, Politics 1, Rituals 2

Gifts: (1) Catfeet [as the Level Three lupus Gift], Heightened Senses, Hare's Leap, Persuasion, Silence; (2) Blissful Ignorance, Eyes of the Cat [as the Level Three metis Gift], Spirit of the Fray; (3) Great Leap, Pulse of the Invisible

Rage: 3; **Gnosis:** 5; **Willpower:** 6

Attacks: Bite (6 dice), claw (6 dice)

Roleplaying Hints: The Bagheera Spy is a living piece of the night born into black leopard form. He prowls the urban jungle and the local wilderness with equal ease, although he longs for a territory he can truly call his own. He's well aware that a local sept of werewolves is in the area, and tries to avoid the "dogs" as much as possible — however, his curiosity often leads him to investigate problems that the local Garou are checking out as well. He isn't a creature of high-tech equipment or surveillance devices — he prefers to observe firsthand, concealed in the shadows. He does not hate werewolves as fervently as his late mentor did, but he still resents them and has no desire to see them do well for themselves.

Corax

If the Garou have anything close to actual friends remaining among the Fera, those friends would be the Corax. The wereravens never approved of the War of Rage, but were largely spared during the war. Many tribes, including the Get of Fenris and Fianna looked the other way while the Corax escaped. In return, the wereravens have been a little more forgiving than most Fera with regards to the War of Rage. They know that

the current generation isn't responsible for their ancestors' deeds — but they also know that werewolves are creatures with very short tempers, and so they keep their distance.

The Corax's original task was to carry news of the Wyrm from one sept to the next, from Garou to Fera and back. They haven't abandoned that duty, but these days they prefer to be much more discreet. They send their warnings covertly, via anonymous email or by spreading rumors. When the werewolves descend on the threat they've anonymously pointed out, the Corax sit high above the battle in raven form, making sure that the Garou do a thorough job — and helping themselves to some of the leftover carnage after the werewolves leave.

Suggested Traits: Corax are by no means combat machines. They have only three forms: Homid, Corvid (the raven-form), and an ungainly Crinos that can outfight a human but little else. Most Corax prefer not to even consider the idea of getting involved in a bloody brawl; what good would *that* do?

Many Corax are able to harden their feathers, then hurl them like darts while in Crinos form (treat as hurled knives with greater effective range). Their Gifts come in a wide variety, but tend to augment the wereravens' ability to gather information rather than their combat ability. Ragabash and Shadow Lord Gifts are particularly appropriate. Corax are creatures of the sun, not the moon; they do not seem to be vulnerable to silver, and they do not possess auspices. They tend toward high Gnosis, very low Rage and average Willpower; they can frenzy, but their Rage is usually so low that this is a very rare occurrence. The wereraven's Crinos form invokes the Delirium in human witnesses, although to a lesser extent than usual.

Wereravens, of course, fly to get around; in Crinos form, they fly roughly as quickly as a Hispo Garou runs, and are even faster in Corvid. They can step sideways as easily as any werewolf, and are adept at maneuvering through the Umbra. Finally, Corax possess the unusual talent of divining information from corpses. Essentially, a Corax that devours the eyeball of a corpse is able to see the last few minutes of the deceased's life from the deceased's point of view — seeing the unfortunate person's last sight just as they saw it.

Freelance Courier

Attributes: Strength 2 (5), Dexterity 4 (6), Stamina 3 (5), Charisma 3, Manipulation 3 (1), Appearance 2 (1), Intelligence 3, Perception 4, Wits 4

Abilities: Alertness 3, Athletics 1, Dodge 4, Empathy 3, Expression 1, Primal-Urge 1, Streetwise 4, Subterfuge 2, Etiquette 1, Firearms 2, Stealth 4, Computer 4, Investigation 4, Law 1, Linguistics 2, Medicine 1, Occult 3, Politics 1, Rituals 1, Science 2

Gifts: (1) Open Seal, Persuasion, Scent of the True Form, Truth of Gaia; (2) Sense the Unnatural, Sight from Beyond, Taking the Forgotten

Rage: 1; **Gnosis:** 4; **Willpower:** 6

Attacks: Claw (6 dice)

Roleplaying Hints: The Freelance Courier has contacts among the local sept of Garou, but they don't know that he's anything other than a simple well-intentioned Kinfolk to a non-local tribe. He cultivates a skittish demeanor, threatening that if the werewolves try to press-gang him into anything other than messenger duty, he'll be gone in a flash. He may have a contact among the sept that knows his true nature, but having heard plenty of tales about what paranoid Garou do to other shapechangers, that contact is sworn to ultimate secrecy. The Freelance Courier is as sassy as his raven relatives, although he knows better than to tease werewolves too much — that's a job best left for someone better suited to surviving an angry werewolf's claws.

Gurahl

Many human mythologies paint the bear as both savage and gentle, a ferocious warrior and a wise healer at the same time. Such stories have their root in the Gurahl, the werebears. Although the Gurahl possess their share of Rage, they also value wisdom and compassion more than do other shapechanging races. Some say that the werebears were once the Garou's mentors and instructors, teaching the werewolves how to heal as well as harm. Unfortunately, when the War of Rage began, the werebears were too scattered to deal with entire packs of werewolves, and very nearly vanished into extinction.

Only a handful of werebears survive today, and most of those have been in a supernatural hibernation for years — sometimes even centuries. As the Apocalypse's final battles draw nearer, more and more of the werebears are awakening. Although the entire race is no larger than a single Garou tribe, they are still honor-bound to try and save Gaia as best they can, fulfilling their ancient duty as healers. Unfortunately, some young Gurahl, upon learning of their race's hard times, swear revenge rather than forgiveness.

The Gurahl almost never appear to the Garou — they remember too many tales of slaughter. Nonetheless, a few septs have deputized packs to seek out legends of the old werebears, trying desperately to find and enlist the scant healers that remain. Locating, protecting and enlisting the aid of an actual werebear would be a source of great honor among the septs that have given up on old prejudices — but regrettably, so few Gurahl survive that the task seems a near impossibility.

Suggested Traits: Gurahl have the full range of five forms, and are generally very strong and tough — if slow — in most of them. An angry werebear is strong enough to uproot trees, even if he doesn't move very quickly. Gurahl do not spend Rage to gain extra actions — each Rage point they spend adds an extra dot to their Strength for a turn. The werebears' Gifts focus on healing and health; powers that preserve life or make one stronger are good choices. Werebears may be of any auspice, although the more "hot-headed" moon signs tend to be younger and the more serene auspices are usually older.

Gurahl have strong Rage and Gnosis, and notably high Willpower. They are not particularly Umbrally adept, requiring a special rite to step sideways. Their Gifts tend toward healing and support; Theurge Gifts are particularly appropriate, although a Gurahl will have Gifts of her auspice list. The race is highly ritualistic, and most werebears know at least a few rites; many devote significantly more attention to rites than to Gifts.

Gurahl breed with three major types of bear: black bears, brown bears and polar bears. (The rarer breeds such as spectacled bears seem to have no Gurahl Kin among them, and pandas aren't compatible with the Gurahl at all.)

Forest Guardian

Attributes: Strength 4 (9), Dexterity 2 (1), Stamina 4 (9), Charisma 4, Manipulation 3 (0), Appearance 2 (0), Intelligence 4, Perception 3, Wits 2

Abilities: Alertness 1, Brawl 4, Dodge 1, Empathy 4, Expression 3, Intimidation 3, Primal-Urge 4, Animal Ken 4, Crafts 3, Leadership 2, Melee 1, Performance 1, Survival 5, Enigmas 4, Investigation 1, Linguistics 1, Medicine 4, Occult 3, Rituals 5

Gifts: (1) Mother's Touch, Razor Claws, Resist Pain, Spirit Speech, Truth of Gaia; (2) Command Spirit, King of the Beasts, Luna's Armor, Snarl of the Predator; (3) Exorcism, Name the Spirit, Reshape Object; (4) Beast Life, Call Elemental, Serenity; (5) Song of the Great Beast, Wall of Granite

Rage: 7; **Gnosis:** 8; **Willpower:** 9

Attacks: Bite (10 dice), claw (10 dice)

Roleplaying Hints: The Forest Guardian fell into a mystical hibernation two hundred years ago, and has recently awoken to find his forest overrun with tourists, outdoor enthusiasts and surveyors. He's a walking anachronism, one more suited to dealing with the early 18th century than the 21st. He struggles to understand the humans that are now so numerous in his sacred land, but they are slowly making his Rage grow. This mighty elder doesn't trust Garou, and it will take a major effort to make him reveal his presence to anyone he suspects of being so much as werewolf Kin.

Mokolé

The Mokolé are also called "the Dragon Breed," and for good reason. Although these shapeshifters breed with crocodilians and monitor lizards, their war forms are colossal monsters as much dinosaur or dragon as anything else. Such is the birthright of the Memory of Gaia; the Mokolé have no fixed Crinos form, but each one instead takes a form that they "remember" from long, long ago.

The Mokolé were especially hard-hit during the War of Rage — many Garou saw the reptilian shapechangers as too close to the Wyrm's image to be coincidental. As a result, the Dragon Breed has a deep grudge against the werewolves, and many react with violence if they find werewolves trespassing in their territory. They aren't urban creatures, and most gather in areas where their reptile Kin flourishes; most American Mokolé live in the southern swamplands where the alligators are. They're social creatures, and although they don't form packs, they do gather in small groups to defend what few caerns are left to them.

Most werewolves go their whole lives without even hearing of a living Mokolé. For their part, the crocodile-shifters are well aware of the Garou's continued existence, and they are happy to stay well clear of any territory that might boast werewolves. A Garou pack is likely to cross a Mokolé's path only in gator or croc country; it's possible that a group of elders might send a pack on a peacemaking mission, but only if they wouldn't mind never seeing that pack again. It's also possible that werewolves working to save a patch of wetlands from being drained might find an unexpected ally in the form of a Mokolé, but the situation would have to be truly dire for the dragon-shifter to reveal itself to its ancestral enemy.

Suggested Traits: Mokolé aren't generally fast, but they make up for it in size and strength. They have only three forms — human, reptile (usually alligator or crocodile, but monitor lizards and even Gila monsters are possible) and Crinos. A Mokolé's Crinos form is highly variable; no two are alike. Each werecrocodile's form is a powerful amalgam of various dinosaur traits, usually towering up to 12 feet long or even larger. They may possess horns, claws, armor, long Tyrannosaur teeth — roughly one unusual trait per Gnosis point.

Mokolé have auspices that are based on the sun's position at the time of their birth (or hatching), but that are otherwise similar to Garou's auspices. Their Gifts are quite varied; a selection of Ahroun, Philodox and Children of Gaia Gifts might represent a Mokolé warrior. They don't possess many Gifts, however; they are hesitant to rely too much on magic. Their ability to remember things that their ancestors saw is quite remarkable; each Mokolé has the equivalent of the Philodox Gift: Wisdom of the Ancient Ways. They have difficulty stepping sideways, and require a special Level Three Gift to do so.

Wetlands Biologist

Attributes: Strength 3 (7), Dexterity 3 (2), Stamina 4 (8), Charisma 3, Manipulation 2 (0), Appearance 3 (0), Intelligence 2, Perception 3, Wits 3

Abilities: Alertness 1, Athletics 4 (swimming), Brawl 2, Empathy 1, Primal-Urge 2, Streetwise 1, Subterfuge 1, Animal Ken 3, Crafts 1, Drive 2, Stealth 2, Survival 2, Computer 1, Investigation 1, Law 2, Linguistics 2, Medicine 3, Politics 2, Rituals 2, Science 4

Gifts: (1) Beast Speech, Fatal Flaw, Razor Claws (used on her horn), Resist Pain; (2) Awe, Clap of Thunder, Luna's Armor

Rage: 6; **Gnosis:** 5; **Willpower:** 7

Attacks: Bite (8 dice), horn (8 dice), tail lash (8 dice bashing)

Roleplaying Hints: The Wetlands Biologist is a strange mix of past and present; although a child of the modern world with a good scientific education, she can see thousands of years into the past thanks to her inherited memories. She spends much of her time doing research in the field, where she also keeps up with her alligator Kin and the occasional fellow Mokolé. She is idealistic and proud, and has sabotaged more than one team of humans trying to drain her swamps or dump toxic waste there. She has never met a werewolf, and although she'd like to be open-minded about the Garou, she has vivid memories of dying at a werewolf's claws. She is gentle and friendly to those she considers on her side, but bitter and vicious to those she considers enemies. In her Crinos form, she resembles a streamlined reptile shaped like a seal, with long Triceratops-like horns and clawed flippers. Her back is heavily plated, and her tail is thick and flexible like an alligator's. In this form, she is clumsy on land but remarkably swift and dangerous when swimming.

Nagah

To the Garou — in fact, to virtually every last one of the Fera — the Nagah are a myth. As far as everyone else is concerned, the wereserpents survive only in Indian legends of the Naga, shapeshifting water-serpents that guard treasures at the bottoms of riverbeds. However, the Nagah managed to survive the War of Rage, and these poisonous creatures have carefully preserved the secret of their continued survival for generations. It is a cardinal sin among the Nagah for a wereserpent to reveal his existence to another shapeshifter (or supernatural being of any kind). Those who violate this rule are harshly punished — and any witnesses are either eliminated or magically compelled to forget they ever saw the Nagah in the first place. Even the spirit world cannot reveal the existence of the wereserpents, for those spirits who do know of the Nagah are compelled to remain silent on the matter.

In their war forms, Nagah resemble giant cobras with barrel chests and powerful, clawed arms; their hoods are often scarred in ritualistic patterns. They breed with poisonous snakes only, preferably cobras.

The Nagah consider themselves the self-appointed police force among shapeshifters. According to their legends, it is their Gaia-appointed role to punish the worst criminals of any Changing Breed — at least, those that are not punished by their own kind. A Gurahl who torments rather than heals, Garou who make war on the innocent instead of the enemy, Bastet who use their gained knowledge to benefit the Wyrm or Weaver — these are the Nagah's targets. They always operate in twos or threes; the wereserpents are apparently too paranoid to work alone.

Suggested Traits: Nagah are swift and strong, almost a match for Garou. Their poison is exceptionally deadly — although there's only enough for about three injections or so, a good dose from a Crinos-form Nagah does seven health levels of aggravated damage (which werecreatures can soak). They can shift into five forms, but only use Homid, Crinos and their cobra form regularly.

Like most other shapeshifters, they have Rage and use it in the usual fashion. Their Gifts tend to focus on stealth and detection, although they also have plenty of Gifts that sharpen their killing powers. Uktena Gifts are particularly appropriate, as are any Gifts taught by snake-spirits. Nagah are able to breathe underwater when in their Crinos or Hispo-like forms.

Trio of Assassins

Attributes: Strength 2 (5), Dexterity 4 (6), Stamina 3 (5), Charisma 3, Manipulation 3 (0), Appearance 3 (0), Intelligence 3, Perception 3, Wits 3

Abilities: Alertness 1, Athletics 1, Brawl 3, Dodge 3, Empathy 1, Primal-Urge 2, Subterfuge 4, Etiquette 3, Firearms 2, Melee 3, Performance 3, Stealth 4, Enigmas 2, Investigation 3, Law 3, Linguistics 2, Politics 3, Rituals 1

Gifts: (1) Heightened Senses, Fatal Flaw, Mother's Touch, Scent of Running Water, Sense Wyrm, Shroud; (2) Blissful Ignorance, Luna's Armor, Sense of the Prey, Spirit of the Fish, Veil of the Wani [which allows Nagah to wipe out an opponent's memory of an encounter with the Nagah as if they suffered from the Delirium; it costs two Gnosis]; (3) Coup de Grace, Eye of the Cobra, Invisibility, Paralyzing Stare; (4) Open Wounds, Whelp Body

Rage: 3; **Gnosis:** 5; **Willpower:** 6

Attacks: Bite (6 dice), claw (6 dice)

Roleplaying Hints: The Trio of Assassins shouldn't even enter a chronicle unless a particular shapechanger is horribly betraying his duty and no others of his kind are able to stop him (or even learn of his treason). When the trio arrives, they do their best to kill the target as quietly as possible, without leaving any trace of their presence (but revealing evidence of their target's wrongdoing). They are trained to strike without hesitation, but they do not enjoy killing — only by regretting the necessity of each death they deliver can they keep themselves from becoming prideful and corrupt. However, the solitude of their task makes them terribly lonely, and they might be tempted to break their code and socialize with the players' characters for just a brief moment, so long as they are able to keep their true identities completely secret.

Nuwisha

Although few Garou have anything even close to proof that the werecoyotes still exist, most wouldn't be surprised if they found out that a few managed to hold on. The Nuwisha are children of Coyote, and emulate their Trickster patron in more ways than

one. Old Uktena and Wendigo tales hold that they were the Laughter of Gaia, put on the earth in order to lighten others' burdens and teach the foolish lessons. Of course, the Nuwisha share Old Man Coyote's sense of troublemaking and mischief, and get into plenty of trouble for following their instincts instead of their brains.

The Nuwisha can handle themselves in a fight, but they're not very warlike next to the Garou. They handle their affairs by stealth, like an entire species of Ragabash. The most clever among their ranks are even able to disguise themselves as werewolves in order to covertly attend Garou moots.

When a werewolf's path crosses that of a werecoyote, it's usually an instance where the Nuwisha has decided to teach the werewolf a lesson. The Nuwisha carefully studies her target, observing the werewolf and noting all his greatest flaws. When she pulls a trick, it's one designed to expose the werewolf's flaws of character and hopefully embarrass him sufficiently that he mends his ways. Of course, she also reserves some pranks for the Wyrm's servitors — such pranks are usually more deadly than instructive, leaving behind a lesson for others along the lines of "don't do what this stupid dead bastard did."

Suggested Traits: All Nuwisha are Ragabash, and should be treated as such. They have no metis, and their Willpower is often average at best. They are small and lithe, comparatively speaking; their Crinos forms are only as large as a werewolf's Glabro. (Modify their forms to reflect an increased Dexterity, but with Strength and Stamina bonuses that are quite modest in comparison to the Garou's forms.) Nuwisha don't possess Rage, and cannot frenzy; however, silver causes them no particular problems. Their Gifts focus on trickery and Umbral travel.

Young Infiltrator

Attributes: Strength 2 (4), Dexterity 4 (7), Stamina 2 (5), Charisma 3, Manipulation 4 (2), Appearance 3 (0), Intelligence 2, Perception 3, Wits 4

Abilities: Alertness 2, Athletics 2, Brawl 1, Dodge 3, Empathy 2, Expression 2, Subterfuge 4, Crafts 1, Etiquette 1, Performance 3, Stealth 3, Enigmas 1, Investigation 1, Linguistics 3, Politics 3, Rituals 1

Gifts: (1) Open Seal, Scent of Running Water, Persuasion, Spirit Speech, Tagalong; (2) Blissful Ignorance, Distractions, Taking the Forgotten; (3) Grasp the Beyond [lower rank for Nuwisha], Great Leap

Gnosis: 5; **Willpower:** 6

Attacks: Bite (5 dice), claw (5 dice)

Roleplaying Hints: The Young Infiltrator has decided to "blend in" with the local werewolves, for reasons of her own. She has spent enough time watching the locals to understand who might be the most sympathetic to her feigned plight, and how best to phrase her cover story. She might even take a particular interest in the players' pack, choosing to offer her "mentorship" to them, or even to tempt one of the pack members into a clandestine roll in the hay. (Nuwisha/Garou unions are never fertile, but there's no reason to let a potential partner know that he *isn't* breaking the Litany....) Once she's gotten into position to pull a trick that points out one of the local sept's major weaknesses, she'll do so and promptly vanish, leaving the werewolves to puzzle out just what went wrong and how they can fix it. Then again, if she's discovered — no disguise is perfect, after all — she might have to leave early. Werewolves don't have much by way of a sense of humor....

Ratkin

The story goes that once Gaia entrusted the care of humanity to the children of Rat, who ate up surplus grain in order to control human population. When the Garou decided to take over the job of shepherding humanity, they came into conflict with the Ratkin. The Ratkin lost the War of Rage — but they survived. Now the wererats are bitter and hateful, gathering in urban warrens and awaiting the day that they can get back at werewolves and humans alike.

Almost all Ratkin are urban, although they don't like the cities all that much — to the Ratkin point of view, the Weaver should be bombed back into the Stone Age so that the world doesn't fall into her clutches. Ratkin have a love/hate relationship with their urban warrens — cities are the best place for rats to survive, but they reek of the Weaver. Most Ratkin have a very low estimation of human life; to many elders, it would be most desirable to eliminate 90% or so of the human population so that the remainder could live well without taking up too much space. As a result, the Ratkin are masters of pestilence, sabotage and assassination. There's no weapon too dirty for a wererat on a mission.

Ratkin are almost never helpful to or supportive of Garou, although they have a grudging respect for the Bone Gnawers (who, after all, follow the same totem). Most Ratkin that werewolves are likely to encounter are parties of wererat assassins bent on revenge — or bands of terrorists and saboteurs dedicated to destroying as much Weaver-stuff as possible.

Suggested Traits: Ratkin have only three forms: Homid, Crinos and Rodens. They are only marginally stronger than humans in their Crinos form, but they're notably quick and tough. Individual Ratkin may be of any auspice save Galliard (the bards of the Ratkin died in the War of Rage, and their lore was lost). Metis are fairly common in the tribe. A Ratkin's Gifts are often tailored to create maximum chaos or to take advantage of an urban environment (Ragabash and Bone Gnawer Gifts are particularly appropriate). Fang daggers are popular weapons among wererats, as are vicious modern fetish weapons such as chainsaws and power drills.

Anti-Weaver Saboteur

Attributes: Strength 2 (3), Dexterity 4 (8), Stamina 4 (5), Charisma 1 (0), Manipulation 3, Appearance 2 (0), Intelligence 3, Perception 3, Wits 4

Abilities: Athletics 2, Brawl 1, Dodge 4, Expression 1, Intimidation 3, Streetwise 4, Subterfuge 3, Crafts 3, Drive 1, Firearms 1, Melee 2, Stealth 4, Survival (urban) 2, Computer 1, Investigation 3, Linguistics 1, Politics 1, Science 3

Gifts: (1) Blur of the Milky Eye, Control Simple Machine, Resist Toxin, Sense Wyrm; (2) Curse of Hatred, Snarl of the Predator [chittering rather than an actual snarl]

Rage: 5; **Gnosis:** 5; **Willpower:** 6

Attacks: Bite (4 dice), fang dagger, portable rotary saw (8 dice aggravated)

Roleplaying Hints: This Ratkin is, to put it politely, on the edge. He runs a very real danger of frenzy at any moment, and is subject to panic attacks if things are going against him. He's paranoid to a point, sure that every room is full of security cameras feeding information back to the Weaver. He doesn't like Garou much, having heard plenty of stories about how werewolves like to kill wererats for fun. He *might* help out a pack who's able to convince him that they're on his side (preferably if a Bone Gnawer, who shares his totem, is doing the convincing), but he'll keep his eyes open for a double-cross at all times.

Rokea

The only known aquatic Changing Breed is, unsurprisingly, a predator. The Rokea are weresharks, ferocious creatures that wield their Rage and their physical prowess as weapons against those who'd violate the seas and their denizens. They seem to be one and all shark-born, with no homids or metis among them; this grants them great knowledge of the sea, but comparatively little experience in dealing with people.

Needless to say, Rokea are unlikely to make an appearance in any land-locked chronicle, but if a pack is investigating some trouble along the coast, there's an outside chance that a wereshark (or a slew of them)

might also show up. The weresharks aren't particularly hostile or friendly toward werewolves — the War of Rage obviously didn't reach underwater and the Rokea feel no particular loyalty toward any of the other Fera.

Suggested Traits: Rokea are fighting machines, roughly equal to Garou in combat. They are somewhat ungainly on land, but they are swift and deadly in the water. Their Gifts allow them elemental mastery over the ocean, as well as improved combat prowess (Get of Fenris and Ahroun Gifts are particularly appropriate). They take five forms — Homid, near human, a massive shark-human Crinos, a huge Hispo-like primitive shark, and shark form.

Rokea Vigilante

Attributes: Strength 3 (7), Dexterity 3 (1 on land, 4 in water), Stamina 4 (7), Charisma 2, Manipulation 2 (0), Appearance 2 (0), Intelligence 3, Perception 4, Wits 3

Abilities: Alertness 2, Athletics (Swim) 5, Brawl 4, Dodge 2, Intimidation 2, Primal-Urge 4, Leadership 1, Stealth 3, Survival (ocean) 4, Investigation 2, Linguistics 1, Medicine 2, Rituals 2

Gifts: (1) Beast Speech, Heightened Senses, Resist Pain, Sense Wyrm; (2) Sense of the Prey, Spirit of the Fray, Venom Blood [lower rank for Rokea]; (3) Elemental Favor (water); Gnaw [lower rank for Rokea]

Rage: 7; **Gnosis:** 5; **Willpower:** 7

Attacks: Bite (9 dice), claw (6 dice)

Roleplaying Hints: The Rokea Vigilante has left the ocean to pursue a particular vendetta, most likely against humans who have callously destroyed something important to the weresharks, but possibly against a Garou or other supernatural creature. He has spent years studying the humans, and manages to blend in moderately effectively, although he is still distinctly "dangerous" to the casual observer. He understands human speech well enough, although he tends to make his sentences short, direct and to the point. ("Leave me alone. He is my prey.") Although he is inclined to listen briefly to fellow servants of Gaia (who can prove they are such to his satisfaction), his high Rage means that any who provoke him run the risk of triggering a frenzy. When such a frenzy hits, the wereshark becomes a vicious killing machine, dedicated to nothing more than killing and devouring his foes.

Animals

Below are some examples of animals Garou may encounter; the Storyteller is of course free to extrapolate other critters. The stats listed here are for typical specimens, and can vary based on health, sex and age. Assume that most bite and claw damage is lethal, while kicks, tail slaps and constriction are bashing. For these general templates, assume a Survival rating of 3-4 for their native habitat; for domestic animals assume a rating of 2.

The Beast Courts

Beginning Storytellers are probably asking themselves, "Just what are the Beast Courts, and what exactly did they have to offer that the Stargazers wanted?" That's a fair question.

The Beast Courts of the Emerald Mother are the governing shapeshifter society of Asia, much as the Garou Nation is the preeminent organization of werebeasts in the Western world. However, due to Asia's more variable shapeshifter population (wolves aren't all that populous, for one), the Beast Courts are composed of many shapeshifter races, in particular various subtribes of Corax, Bastet, Mokolé, Garou and Ratkin. Because the War of Rage never reached into Asia, these various Fera have a much easier time getting along with one another (although it's still tense going).

The Beast Courts don't commonly deal with Westerners (whom they call "Sunset People"), although a few emissaries have established diplomatic relations with a few septs in Australia, western North America and the Middle East. These days, those emissaries are more likely to be Stargazers than any other race, as the Beast Courts have found that werewolves respond best to their own kind.

For those interested in learning still more, **Hengeyokai: Shapeshifters of the East** contains a full look at the Beast Courts; although the supplement was published before the Stargazers' inclusion, it still should provide a Storyteller with plenty of material for portraying the Garou and Fera's Eastern cousins.

Canids

Wolf

This represents a good-sized timberwolf. These stats can be modified slightly for a wolfhound.

Attributes: Strength 3, Dexterity 2, Stamina 3, Perception 3, Intelligence 2, Wits 2

Abilities: Alertness 2, Athletics 2, Brawl 3, Dodge 1, Stealth 2

Willpower: 3

Armor Rating: 0

Attacks: Bite (3 dice)

Health Levels: OK, -1, -1, -2, -2, -5, Incapacitated

Coyote

Smaller than a wolf, and more solitary, the coyote is a cunning opportunist. The bane of farmers and ranchers, its high-pitched howl can be heard in fields, woodlots and suburban neighborhoods across much of North America.

Attributes: Strength 2, Dexterity 3, Stamina 2, Perception 3, Intelligence 2, Wits 3

Abilities: Alertness 3, Athletics 2, Brawl 3, Dodge 2, Stealth 2

Willpower: 2

Armor Rating: 0

Attacks: Bite (2 dice)

Health Levels: OK, -1, -2, -2, -5, Incapacitated

Fox

Slightly larger than a housecat, foxes tend to be solitary or travel in mated pairs.

Attributes: Strength 1, Dexterity 3, Stamina 1, Perception 3, Intelligence 2, Wits 2

Abilities: Alertness 3, Athletics 2, Brawl 2, Dodge 3, Stealth 3

Willpower: 2

Armor Rating: 0

Attacks: Bite (2 dice)

Health Levels: OK, -1, -2, -5, Incapacitated.

Hound

This represents a basic kibble-fed hunter. Remember that they run in packs. For trained guard dogs, increase Strength, Stamina, Intimidation and Stealth.

Attributes: Strength 2, Dexterity 2, Stamina 2, Perception 2, Intelligence 2, Wits 1

Abilities: Alertness 2, Athletics 1, Brawl 1, Dodge 1, Intimidation 1, Stealth 1

Willpower: 2 (up to 5 for trained or tenacious dog)

Armor Rating: 0

Attacks: Bite (3 dice)

Health Levels: OK, -1, -2, -2, -5, Incapacitated

Felids

Cougar

Includes both western cougar and the eastern/Florida panther. A solitary ambush hunter. Attacks on humans grow more frequent as people encroach on cougar territory.

Attributes: Strength 3, Dexterity 4, Stamina 3, Perception 3, Intelligence 2, Wits 3

Abilities: Alertness 3, Athletics (climbing) 4, Brawl 3, Dodge 2, Intimidation 2, Stealth 3

Willpower: 3

Armor Rating: 0

Attacks: Claw (4 dice), bite (5 dice)

Health Levels: OK, -1, -1, -1, -2. -2, -5, Incapacitated

Lion

The only big cat to live and hunt in large groups (prides). Though males are larger, females do the bulk of the hunting.

Attributes: Strength 4, Dexterity 3, Stamina 3, Perception 3, Intelligence 2, Wits 2

Abilities: Alertness 3, Athletics 2, Brawl 3, Dodge 2, Intimidation 4, Stealth 3

Willpower: 4

Armor Rating: 1

Attacks: Claw (5 dice), bite (6 dice)

Health Levels: OK, OK, -1, -1, -1, -2, -2, -5, Incapacitated

Tiger

The largest of the great cats.

Attributes: Strength 5, Dexterity 3, Stamina 4, Perception 3, Intelligence 3, Wits 2

Abilities: Alertness 3, Athletics 2, Brawl 3, Dodge 2, Intimidation 4, Stealth 4

Willpower: 4

Armor Rating: 1

Attacks: Claw (6 dice), bite (7 dice)

Health Levels: OK, OK, -1, -1, -1, -2, -2, -5, -5, Incapacitated

Ursids

Black Bear

Rarely aggressive in the wild, black bears can be dangerous when raiding garbage or taking handouts

from humans. They generally hibernate in caves or other protected areas during the winter.

Attributes: Strength 4, Dexterity 2, Stamina 4, Perception 3, Intelligence , Wits 2

Abilities: Alertness 3, Athletics 2, Brawl 2, Dodge 1, Intimidation 2, Stealth 2

Willpower: 3

Armor Rating: 1

Attacks: Claw (5 dice), bite (5 dice)

Health Levels: OK, OK, -1, -1, -2, -2, -5, Incapacitated

Brown/Grizzly Bear

Though generally more herbivorous than their smaller cousins, they steal carrion and sometimes hunt and fish. Very aggressive and unpredictable. They hibernate in winter dens.

Attributes: Strength 7, Dexterity 2, Stamina 6, Perception 3, Intelligence 2, Wits 2

Abilities: Alertness 3, Athletics 2, Brawl 3, Intimidation 4, Stealth 1

Willpower: 4

Armor Rating: 2

Attacks: Claw (8 dice), bite (8 dice)

Health Levels: OK, OK, OK, -1, -1, -1, -2, -2, -5, -5, Incapacitated

Polar Bear

Well-adapted to life on the ice, polar bears are patient, relentless opportunists and very dangerous.

Attributes: Strength 7, Dexterity 3, Stamina 7, Perception 4, Intelligence 2, Wits 3

Abilities: Alertness 4, Athletics 3, Brawl 3, Intimidation 4, Stealth 3

Willpower: 5

Armor Rating: 2

Attacks: Claw (8 dice), Bite (8 dice)

Health Levels: OK, OK, OK, -1, -1, -1, -2, -2, -5, -5, Incapacitated

Herbivores

Deer

Includes medium sized deer such as whitetails and fallow.

Attributes: Strength 2, Dexterity 3, Stamina 3, Perception 3, Intelligence 1, Wits 2

Abilities: Alertness 3, Athletics 2, Brawl 2, Dodge 3, Stealth 2

Willpower: 2

Armor Rating: 0

Attacks: Kick (2 dice), antler charge (bucks in season, 4 dice)

Health Levels: OK, -1, -1, -2, -2, -5, Incapacitated

Elk/Red Deer

Include medium to large deer (moose would be larger still).

Attributes: Strength 4, Dexterity 2, Stamina 4, Perception 2, Intelligence 1, Wits 2

Abilities: Alertness 2, Athletics 3, Brawl 2, Dodge 2, Stealth 2

Willpower: 2

Armor Rating: 1

Attacks: Kick (4 dice), antler charge (bucks in season, 5 dice)

Health Levels: OK, OK, -1, -1, -1, -2, -2, -5, Incapacitated

Bison

The largest living wild ox. Travels in woodlands and plains, in herds ranging from a dozen or so to thousands.

Attributes: Strength 8, Dexterity 2, Stamina 6, Perception 2, Intelligence 1, Wits 2

Abilities: Alertness 1, Athletics 2, Brawl 3, Dodge 1

Willpower: 3

Armor Rating: 1

Attacks: Head butt (8 dice), gore (9 dice), kick (7 dice)

Health Levels: OK, OK, OK, -1, -1, -2, -2, -5, -5, Incapacitated

Domestic Bull

Attributes: Strength 7, Dexterity 2, Stamina 5, Perception 2, Intelligence 1, Wits 1

Abilities: Alertness 1, Athletics 2, Brawl 1, Dodge 1

Willpower: 2

Armor Rating: 1

Attacks: Gore (8 dice), Kick (6 dice)

Health Levels: OK, OK, -1, -1, -1, -2, -2, -2, -5, Incapacitated

Horse

Represents a riding horse; draft horses will be stronger.

Attributes: Strength 5, Dexterity 3, Stamina 4, Perception 2, Intelligence 2, Wits 3

Abilities: Alertness 2, Athletics 3, Brawl 2, Dodge 2

Willpower: 3

Armor Rating: 0

Attacks: Kick (5 dice), bite (2 dice)

Health Levels: OK, OK, -1, -1, -1, -2, -2, -5, Incapacitated

Reptilians

Alligator/Crocodile

Stats are for a large (10' or so) alligator; Nile and saltwater crocodiles may be a good deal larger and stronger. A favored tactic is to ambush and drag prey into the water, where they spin until victim is knocked senseless. Both crocodilians can shut down their systems and lay on a river bottom for an hour or more without coming up for air.

Attributes: Strength 4, Dexterity 2, Stamina 4, Perception 2, Intelligence 1, Wits 2

Abilities: Alertness 2, Athletics 1, Brawl 2, Stealth 3

Willpower: 2

Armor Rating: 2

Attacks: Bite (5 dice), spin (6 dice/turn + drowning effects), tail slap (4 dice)

Health Levels: OK, OK, -1, -1, -2, -2, -5, Incapacitated

Viper

This includes vipers such as puff adders as well as pit vipers like rattlesnakes, water moccasins, bushmasters, and the fer-de-lance. Usually well camouflaged and stocky, they tend to wait for prey to come to them. Pit vipers have heat-sensitive heat organs in front of

Snake Venom Rules

If a character gets herself bitten, it will likely be more than an annoyance. Venom doesn't act instantly; for more realism, draw out the damage. If the poison inflicts seven health levels, for example, take one health level per half hour; for a powerful elaphid (e.g. mamba), make it one health level every five or ten minutes. Soak rolls are possible; the difficulty varies from 5 (a small copperhead) to 9 (a taipan or other highly lethal snake). The proper antivenin, taken quickly, reduces the difficulty of the soak roll by 2.

Even if the victim manages to soak the worst of the venom, she will still be in pain. If she tangles with a taipan or a mamba, for example, the poison may send her into respiratory arrest in a matter of minutes. A large diamondback may give her a scar for life. Damage may not be healed until the poison has run its course or been neutralized.

each eye, which they use to track prey. Viper poison is primarily hemotoxic, destroying blood vessels and tissues, and is delivered through two long fangs that snap into ready position during the strike. As with many snakes, they retain a striking reflex for minutes or even hours after death.

Attributes: Strength 0, Dexterity 2, Stamina 2, Perception 1, Intelligence 1, Wits 2

Abilities: Alertness 3, Brawl 3, Intimidation 2, Stealth 3

Willpower: 2

Armor Rating: 0

Attacks: Bite (2 dice + poison. If damage gets through armor — including heavy clothing or thick hide — the victim takes no actual damage from the bite itself, but must soak damage according to the amount and strength of the poison; a copperhead might do four health levels while a larger diamondback might do eight or more. Vipers may strike multiple times.)

Health Levels: OK, -1, -2, Dead

Cobras

Cobras and other elaphids (from coral snakes to taipans and mambas) are quick and deadly. Their fangs are short and fixed, so they often bite and chew their venom into a wound. Their poison is predominately neurotoxic, resulting in paralysis and breathing problems.

Attributes: Strength 1, Dexterity 3, Stamina 2, Perception 1, Intelligence 1, Wits 2

Abilities: Alertness 3, Brawl 2, Stealth 2

Willpower: 2

Armor Rating: 0

Attacks: Bite (1 die + poison; if damage gets through armor — including heavy clothing or thick hide — the victim must soak damage according to the amount and strength of the poison; a coral snake might do three health levels (for a very small amount of venom) while a taipan or mamba might do 10 or more. The really bad part is that some snakes, such as the taipan, have a habit of multiple strikes).

Health Levels: OK, -1, -2, -5, Dead

Giant Constrictor

Covers anacondas, pythons and boas. Depending on species, these snakes can grow up to 30 feet long. Camouflaged with mottled patterns, these snakes wait patiently for prey to come into range. Then they grab, coil around, and suffocate their dinner. Seldom attack anything they can't swallow whole, but their jaws unhinge to take in larger prey. These stats reflect a good-sized anaconda.

Attributes: Strength 4, Dexterity 2, Stamina 3, Perception 2, Intelligence 1, Wits 2

Abilities: Alertness 2, Athletics 2, Brawl 2, Stealth 3

Willpower: 2

Armor Rating: 0

Attacks: Bite (2 dice), squeeze (treat as Grapple followed by an extended Strength vs. Strength contest; if the snake wins, treat as suffocation for that turn — **Werewolf**, page 188)

Health Levels: OK, OK, -1, -1, -1, -2, -5, Incapacitated.

Birds

Raven

Very clever scavengers. Quite curious.

Attributes: Strength 1, Dexterity 3, Stamina 2, Perception 3, Intelligence 2, Wits 3

Abilities: Alertness 2, Athletics 2, Brawl 1, Dodge 2

Willpower: 2

Armor Rating: 0

Attacks: Peck (1 die)

Health Levels: OK, -1, -2, -5, Dead

Hawk/Owl

Typical birds of prey. Both have sharp vision, but hawks are daylight hunters while owls fly by night. Hawks have incredible vision, while owls, in addition to excellent night vision, can locate the faintest sound with pinpoint accuracy.

Attributes: Strength 1, Dexterity 3, Stamina 2, Perception 4, Intelligence 1, Wits 2

Abilities: Alertness 3, Athletics 2, Brawl 2, Dodge 2

Willpower: 3

Armor Rating: 0

Attacks: Claw (2 dice; 4 dice if diving), peck (1 die)

Health Levels: OK, -1, -2, -5, Dead

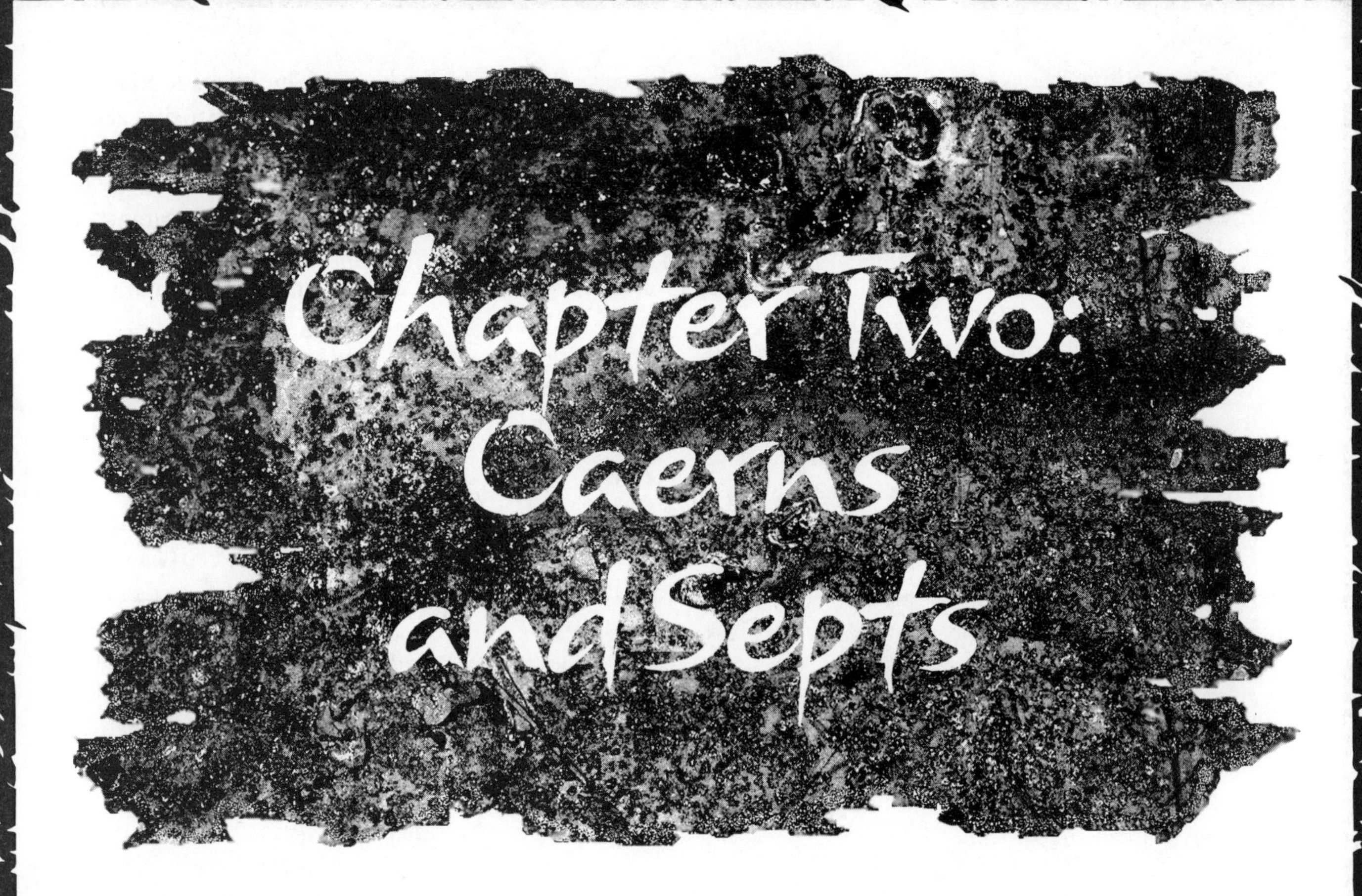

The caern and sept should be the heart of most **Werewolf** games — they are a means to dramatically illustrate the primitive society of the Garou; they represent everything that werewolves are willing to fight, bleed and die for; they are the closest thing that werewolves have to a true home.

There isn't enough room in this book to detail caerns and septs thoroughly from top to bottom (not without taking up the entire book and then some). However, the following information should prove useful enough for you to get a chronicle started. If you want even more detail, the **Werewolf Players Guide** and **Guardians of the Caerns** offer as much information as you could ask for.

Caerns

A caern is more than a simple reservoir of Gnosis — it is the spiritual center of Garou society. They are sacred areas, rich with Umbral energy. It's impossible to stand in the center of a caern and be unaware of the spirit energy that pulses all around you. Caerns can change a person's very way of thought.

As Storyteller, you want to design your chronicle's caern to complement the sort of game you want to run. If you plan to run an intense game of dark horror and shadowy morals, you probably want a caern that exudes strength and ruthlessness, not compassion and warmth. If you want to play up the savage nature of the World of Darkness' wilderness, the caern should be physically foreboding. The mood you evoke in your players as you describe life at the caern will color the entire game; it's worth some extra thought.

The Physical Territory

A caern covers a lot of area. Not all of this area is the low-Gauntlet power source that feeds the Garou; a proper caern also needs living space for its defenders, room to set up adequate defensive lines, and other necessities for the sept.

Everything is built around the caern's *heart*. This area is not necessarily at the geographic center of the caern, but it must be defensible. The caern's heart is a place where the Umbra and physical world are one — there is no Gauntlet here, and the world is a fusion of Penumbra and physical realm. The heart might be a circle of standing stones, the depths of a cave, an ancient tree, an old urban theater, virtually anything. The sept leaders often call meetings at the heart, and this is the place where the sept calls on the caern totem or opens the caern's powers. A rare few caerns actually have two hearts: the Central Park Caern of New York City is one example. These caerns are rare indeed, and usually occur only when the area of the bawn contains two strongholds of spiritual power, each one distinct in nature from the other. (The Central Park Caern, for instance, has one heart that draws on the energy of the water that runs throughout the city, and another that feeds on the spiritual energy of the massive numbers of people in the city.)

By contrast, the *bawn* is the caern's outer boundary; this may range from a city block or two in an urban caern to a miles-wide swath of wilderness. Werewolves can sense when they step across the boundary of a bawn; humans and other intruders cannot (although the retaliatory attacks of the sept's territorial residents usually inform them of their intrusion). Many werewolves live inside the bawn — those who can, at any rate. For many Garou, necessity demands they live elsewhere. Kinfolk generally live outside the bawn, but close by.

Since Garou have nowhere else safe to meet, they commonly set aside an *assembly area* within the caern's bawn to hold their moots, welcome guests, try criminals, and so on. These places may be natural clearings or hollows, or in the case of urban caerns, large warehouses or amphitheaters.

To honor their fallen, Garou also set aside an area of remembrance, commonly called the *Graves of the Hallowed Heroes*. This area isn't always a literal graveyard; usually it's simply a memorial area with tokens of all the caern's fallen defenders where werewolves can go to meditate. Here Garou make peace with their ancestors — or prepare themselves before battle to join them.

Caerns often have other areas particular to each individual caern. A Glass Walker caern might have an armory of munitions to be used just in case claws and fetishes aren't enough; a Children of Gaia caern might have a lodge where the sept members can rendezvous with their Kinfolk mates. Consider adding at least one area peculiar to your chronicle's caern to add extra character.

The Umbrascape

The caern's physical territory should reflect the nature of the caern itself, but this is even truer with a caern's Penumbral landscape. The spirits found in a caern's Umbrascape should be appropriate to the caern's purpose and tribal affinity; the very landscape should reflect the caern's type. Garou are expected to be particularly respectful of a caern's spirit inhabitants, as they are extensions of the caern and its purpose. Each area within the caern tends to have a particular resonance within the Penumbra; for example, the Graves of the Hallowed Heroes may be particularly still and cool in the Penumbra, while the assembly area may have a pronounced echo.

Caern Powers

A caern's type determines the kind of power it can lend to its protectors via the Rite of Opened Caern. As described under that rite and on the Caerns chart (**Werewolf**, pg. 226), success grants the ritemaster extra dice on actions related to the caern's affinity. The ritemaster may distribute these dice among other individuals as he sees fit; each individual retains these bonus dice for the remainder of the day. Each caern can grant its powers only a few times each day; in game terms, a caern can grant powers through the Rite of the Opened Caern only once per day for every level of the caern. (A level two caern can grant power only twice each day before it must recharge its energy, and so on.)

Sample Caern Ranks

The following figures approximate the general size, capabilities and other details of caerns by rank. These guidelines are *very* general; Storytellers are completely within their rights to modify any and all offered statistics as appropriate. Caerns are, after all, *so* rare that they're almost impossible to pigeonhole.

Rank 1:

Average Population: 4-10 Garou

Average Bawn: 200 acres or (usually much) less

Maximum Moon Bridge Distance: 1,000 miles

Gauntlet: 4

Disadvantages: Very little raw power; smaller bawn size means almost no area for lupus to live.

Advantages: Fewer Garou to compete with; little interpack politics; good possibility of a player character filling one of the sept positions; the Wyrm's forces are probably unaware of its existence.

Rank 2:

Average Population: 8-15 Garou

Average Bawn: 350 acres

Maximum Moon Bridge Distance: 2,000 miles

Gauntlet: 4

Disadvantages: Not many powers; limited room; not as many defenders.

Advantages: Still little politicking; packs have access to healthy totem spirits.

Rank 3:

Average Population: 10-20 Garou

Average Bawn: 800 acres

Maximum Moon Bridge Distance: 3,000 miles

Gauntlet: 3

Disadvantages: Little chance for filling a sept role; large enough that defense is a bigger concern; the Wyrm has definitely taken notice; starting to become difficult to maintain or expand.

Advantages: Real source of potent power; strong allies in septmates; easy access to teachers and spirits.

Rank 4:

Average Population: 15-30 Garou

Average Bawn: 800 acres

Maximum Moon Bridge Distance: 6,000 miles

Gauntlet: 3

Disadvantages: More people than room; Wyrm is actively trying to destroy the caern; much interpack and tribal politics; limited access to resources.

Advantages: Very potent caern with a multitude of powers, mighty allies and mentors.

Rank 5:

Average Population: 25-40 Garou

Average Bawn: 1,000 or more acres

Maximum Moon Bridge Distance: 10,000 miles

Gauntlet: 2

Disadvantages: Typically huge bawn; as large a population of werewolves sharing resources as can be; sept leaders tend to ignore pups; Wyrmspawn are constantly planning or launching attacks; cannot be hidden.

Advantages: Huge numbers of Garou come to defend it.

Caern Totems

A sept doesn't choose its caern totem — the totem chooses the caern. The caern totem is a spirit that in some way epitomizes the land itself, the energies of the caern and the sept of Garou that calls it. The Rite of Caern Building sends out a "call" that is answered by an appropriate spirit; many septs have been surprised to have their call answered by a totem somewhat unlike the one they were expecting. The caern totem in time attracts small broods of like-minded Gafflings, who serve as the messengers and Umbral sentries of the caern totem.

Caern totems are directly tied to their caerns — they cannot roam the Umbra, and they suffer any damage done to their land as well. Their pact with the sept is doubly important because of this dependence; the totem needs the sept to defend its lands and health, and in return it will offer the Garou the power that the caern has to offer. To betray this trust is a grave offense — yet another reason that the tenet of the Litany forbidding the violation of caerns is the most harshly enforced.

Although a caern totem is pledged to aid the werewolves who care for it, they are not compelled to coddle the sept — in fact, it's usually a poor idea to do so. Unearned power or assistance tends to breed arrogance and corruption. A caern totem is often cryptic when offering mystic advice, strict when called upon to render judgement, and even demanding when lending martial strength to its sept. Simply being a werewolf is not proof enough that one deserves Gaia's greatest gifts — a Garou must be prepared to work hard and make many sacrifices to earn his birthright.

Caern Totem Statistics

Despite their limitations, caern totems are fairly powerful as spirits go. With their access to the energies of a caern, they have notably high Gnosis ratings; even the bellicose totem of a caern of Rage possesses more Gnosis than other spirits of its ilk. Rage is usually very strongly tied to the caern's type; totems of caerns of Wyld, Strength and other vibrant caern types are more likely to have high Rage than those who protect caerns of Enigmas, Wisdom and other serene places. Willpower is normally rather high, although it depends on the totem's nature; the mouse-spirit totem of an urban caern may be quite timid and reserved despite its great wisdom.

All caern totems should have the Realm Sense Charm; a caern totem will normally be able to detect unusual disturbances across the caern's borders, although as always it must make a Gnosis roll to perceive specifics. Materialize is uncommon but not necessary. Other Charms should reflect the spirit's nature and that of its domain; the totem of a caern situated on a lake is far more likely to possess Flood than Create Fires.

Local Spirits

Inside the bawn, many of the local spirits are awake and aware — a werewolf is far more likely to encounter an awakened oak-spirit within a caern's

boundaries than without. The Rite of Caern Building sends forth ripples of energy, often awakening many spirits in the vicinity as well as attracting a caern totem. And, of course, werewolves often use the Rite of Spirit Awakening to gain further allies and instructors within the caern's boundaries.

The spirits of a caern generally offer sept members greater respect and friendship than would otherwise be the case — the sept has usually earned it. If the Storyteller chooses, when a sept member negotiates with one of the caern totem's brood (such as to persuade the spirit to teach a Gift or empower a fetish), the difficulty of all Social rolls is lowered by 1. Newly changed cubs don't always receive this reward; they must have served the sept faithfully and well for several moons before the spirits treat them as full brethren.

Septs

As important as caerns are, the task of protecting them from corruption or destruction is a heavy responsibility. The structure of the sept arose from this very responsibility — a sept is as much a military unit as it is a social unit or settlement. Sept structure has evolved slowly and always according to what is necessary to guarding the caerns of the world; the many multitribal septs of the modern age are a compromise established to more effectively fight the Garou's longstanding war.

Even though the sept is organized for defense, it is still a social unit as well. Werewolves are pack creatures; like wolves and humans, they function at their best when among their own kind. When constructing a sept for your chronicle, be sure to keep this social aspect in mind. Although it's important that the sept is logically strong enough to hold a caern, you also want to offer your players plenty of opportunity for roleplaying, whether it's playing political games to advance their pet agendas among the elders or forging bonds of filial devotion with foster parents.

Not all werewolves spend all their time within the bawn's boundaries. At any given time, roughly half of the sept can be expected to remain at the caern. Fewer, and the caern would be dangerously unguarded; more, and the sept isn't sending enough warriors out to take the fight to the enemy. However, a sept is generally active day or night — the werewolves' enemies aren't strictly diurnal or nocturnal, so the werewolves themselves can't afford to be.

Many Garou don't have human lives any more — they don't have homes to return to, they can't hold down steady jobs, and the enemy is constantly at their heels. These werewolves tend to live in the sept full-time. However, every sept is likely to have some members who are managing to bring in money from the human world one way or another. Even werewolves have to eat. The Garou who continue to live human lives (or a semblance thereof) usually spend roughly two-thirds of their time seeing to their human affairs; the rest of the time belongs to their duty as Garou. Even these routines are secondary to any need that may arise — as a result, most werewolves who work have found "unconventional" jobs with flexible hours, so that they're free to move when needed.

When designing a sept for your chronicle, be sure that you take the characters' background stories (and Backgrounds) into account. If one character has a high level of Mentor, perhaps a ranking sept official is his guardian; if another has several dots in Kinfolk, you should think about where her relatives stay and how they figure into the tribal politics of the sept. Unless you're running a chronicle that focuses on travel or a pack cut off from its support networks, the sept could very well be the focus of your game. It deserves your attention; if done right, it'll certainly capture the attention of your players.

Flavor

A caern's purpose and the mix of tribes that protect it go a long way toward establishing the "feel" of a sept. A caern dedicated to Rage, strength or Primal-Urge will drip with raw intensity — even the mystics guarding such a place will tend to be aggressive, powerful figures. By compare, a caern dedicated to enigmas or Gnosis will be a potent force for introspection and visionquesting, where even Ahroun are encouraged to master themselves before going into battle. Or perhaps the caern is dedicated to honor or kingship, and thus is a focal point for the politics of many septs. A caern dedicated to hope or fertility should be the rarest of all, and all the more vulnerable because the entire war is against it.

Similarly, the tribes represented at the sept — and the ratio of their numbers — will play a large part in establishing the sept's flavor. Virtually no sept has members of *every* tribe — werewolves are just too few these days. However, the desperate nature of the times means that tribes who historically have been at each other's throats are sometimes forced to cooperate — the Get of Fenris and Black Furies, Fianna and Wendigo, even the Red Talons and Glass Walkers. The tension between these tribes can lead to a number of plot hooks and a very intense game environment; only the need to defend the caern prevents outright war from breaking out.

The sept's tribal structure will probably be influenced by your players' choice of characters; if two players want to play Get of Fenris, that's a good argument for a strong Fenrir presence in the sept. Don't let a player browbeat you into making his character's tribe more powerful in sept politics than you'd like; ultimately, the sept structure is up to you. However, you should be sure that each character will have *somewhere* to learn Gifts, commune with their tribal totem, learn the mysteries of his tribe, and so on.

Finally, don't forget that a tribe is a social unit, not a personality disorder. Despite the very strong influences of breed, auspice and tribe, each werewolf is an individual. Your sept can have forthright Shadow Lords, bellicose Children of Gaia, pacifistic Red Talons, even-tempered Get of Fenris or humble Silver Fangs...but probably not all at once. Who'd believe it?

Sept Offices

Military and social units need structure, and the sept is no different. Werewolves, like wolves, are instinctively inclined toward hierarchy. The sept offices have evolved partly out of this need for hierarchy and partly for maximum efficiency in defending the caerns. The following are the most common offices held by sept members; some large septs may have other, more specialized offices in addition, while small septs may have elders who take on two or more offices at once simply because there's nobody else for the job.

• **Council of Elders** — The Council of Elders is the sept's main ruling body — usually three to 13 elders, depending on the size and prosperity of the sept. The Grand Elder (usually a Philodox) is the voice of the council, although he can be overruled if the council votes against his decrees.

• **Warder** — The Warder is the equivalent of a sept's captain of the guard or head of security — her word is law when it comes to defending the caern proper. Only the most battle-proven elders can rise to this important post. The Warder's authority can even override the Council's in times of danger. The Warder cannot order packs to take missions outside the caern, but she can demand that packs remain behind to guard the caern in times of need.

• **Guardians** — The Guardians are the warriors whose primary duty is to remain behind and guard the caern. Some septs assign this role to as many packs as they can afford to spare from the front lines. Being chosen as a Guardian is a great honor, and those who serve faithfully are rewarded with Honor renown (as well as Glory when called upon to prove themselves in battle).

- **Master of the Rite** — The Master of the Rite monitors all rites performed at the caern; it is her duty to ensure that nobody calls on powers that would be dangerous to unleash within the caern. Her permission is necessary to enact a rite within the bawn, and she usually stays at hand during the rite to make sure nothing goes wrong. Finally, she is responsible for performing most rites that affect the entire caern — caern rites and punishment rites in particular. This office is customarily held by Theurges or Philodox, but can fall to anyone qualified (preferably with Rituals 5 and knowledge of most of the rites in the **Werewolf** rulebook).
- **Gatekeeper** — The Gatekeeper is charged with control over any moon bridges opened in or to the caern. In times of siege, the Gatekeeper usually forbids any access to the caern's moon bridge. His responsibility forbids him from leaving the caern, and his post usually puts him at the heart of any political machinations involving other septs.
- **Keeper of the Land** — The Keeper of the Land is the caern's caretaker, who is entrusted with the duty of keeping the caern's lands well maintained. This post stems from more than vanity — spirits demand respect for themselves and their physical analogues. A tree-spirit whose tree was neglected and fell ill can bear a grudge for centuries afterward. Not all tribes (and their allied spirits) see a need for this office, however; Bone Gnawers and Red Talons in particular prefer a more "honest" bawn.
- **Master of the Challenge** — If one sept member challenges another, the Master of the Challenge oversees the clash. It is his duty to ensure that no duels go too far (although this rule is relaxed in militant septs), and to impartially judge any challenges of gamecraft, riddles or tests of character. This post is quite necessary, as without it many werewolves would surely die in brawls over their honor — preserving their honor, perhaps, but robbing Gaia of more defenders.

Lesser Offices

The following offices are present mainly in larger, more formal septs; most septs these days are too small to spare the warm bodies to hold these posts full-time. It's entirely possible, especially in these days, that one person may hold more than one of the lesser offices or a lesser office in conjunction with a greater one.

The **Master of the Howl**, traditionally a Galliard, leads other Gibbous Moons in the Opening Howl that begins every moot. The role evolved out of a need for the Opening Howl to set precisely the tone for a given moot's business.

The **Caller of the Wyld**, often a Theurge, leads the sept in the various rituals of homage to the pack, tribe and caern totems that watch over the sept. She also specializes in summoning the particular spirits that are allied to the sept. In most modern septs, this office's duties simply fall to the Master of the Rite.

The **Truthcatcher**, almost always a Philodox, mediates disputes and ordains punishments for violations of the Litany or sept law. Serious offenses are always punished at a moot in full view of the entire sept.

The **Talesinger**, of any auspice (but commonly a Galliard), leads the sept in tales of the past during each moot. She may also bring forward other werewolves to play the part of past heroes, reenacting great legends in pantomime to honor the Garou's ancestors.

The **Wyrm Foe**, always a great warrior (and therefore usually an Ahroun) leads the sept in the Revel that concludes each moot. His howl incites the already excited sept to charge through the caern's bawn, savagely killing any intruders they may find there. The Wyrm Foe may also coordinate the activities of packs that strike at the Wyrm's heart away from the sept, passing on information for them to use on their missions. The Master of the Challenge usually assumes this role in smaller septs.

Moots

Although it's possible to tell a story revolving around a moot with just the bare bones information in the **Werewolf** rulebook, a little more detail is always helpful. The following information is meant to help Storytellers customize the moots held at a sept, and to provide a framework that should hopefully inspire a story held at a moot. Those who are interested in even more detail are encouraged to consult the Werewolf Players Guide, and *all* Storytellers are encouraged to tailor moots as much as they like to properly reflect the character of their septs.

Most moots follow a fairly basic pattern, one that has a practical purpose. In order, the five stages of a moot are the Opening Howl, the Inner Sky, Cracking the Bone, Stories and Songs, and the Revel. These stages allow the sept to gather together, honor their totems and recharge the caern, air any grievances, affirm their history and finally give release to their passions. Prop-

erly performed, a moot reaffirms what it means to be Garou in the hearts of all that attend.

• The Opening Howl

All moots begin with the Opening Howl, led by the Master of the Howl. Each sept's howl has a distinctive resonance, blending together the flavor of the caern, the voices of the tribes present and the tone of recent events. This howl is meant to stir the hearts of the participants and set the mood for the moot to come — in times of war, the Opening Howl is grim and resounding, while in times of celebration, it reverberates with joy.

• The Inner Sky

The moot's second portion devotes itself to contacting and honoring the sept's spirit allies, thereby strengthening the caern. The Caller of the Wyld (or Master of the Rite, if no Caller exists) leads the rituals to contact and pay tribute to the spirits. This is a deeply reverent ceremony, if not always serene — the spirits of some caerns prefer being contacted through ritual combat or boisterous music and dance.

• Cracking the Bone

The third stage is the most serious, as this portion of the moot is the portion dedicated to sept business. Here the elders make edicts on sept policy, and sept members air their grievances. Any temporal business, from reports on the Wyrm's movements to financial considerations, is handled during the Cracking of the Bone. Most septs allow anyone with something to say to do so during this time, although those who speak frivolously or out of turn may very well lose Honor. This is also the portion of the moot where the elders mete out punishments against those who've violated sept or Garou law.

• Stories and Songs

Once the formal business is finished, the Talesinger leads the sept in spinning stories of past and present Garou adventures. This stage of the moot is where the Garou acknowledge their septmates' recent deeds of Renown and honor their ancestors with legendary tales. These stories are meant not only to give honor where honor is due, but also to inspire the sept to emulate the glorious achievements of their ancestors and peers.

• **The Revel**

The passion of every Garou in the sept builds toward the Revel, when it finally releases in a burst of tremendous physical, emotional and spiritual intensity. Once the sept is roused as high as possible, the Wyrm Foe assumes Lupus form and gives a mighty howl. The rest of the sept joins in the howl, and Garou not already in Lupus make the change, emulating the Wyrm Foe. Then the Wyrm Foe charges out of the caern proper, leading the entire sept on a run to clear the area around the caern of all enemies. Werewolves in the frenzied throes of the Revel are quite literally the stuff of humans' nightmares.

The Garou passion released during the Revel is effectively raw Gnosis that pours back into the caern itself, sustaining the caern just as it sustains the sept. As the Revel ends, the werewolves find their way back to the caern, exhausted but full of feelings of purpose and unity.

Justice

The modern legal systems of the Western world are a far cry from Garou justice. Werewolves keep their own laws, and punish transgressors as swiftly and severely as the most notorious "hanging judges" of the Old West. Although a werewolf can commit many errors of judgement or lapses in morals that lead to a loss of Renown, some crimes demand more severe retribution.

A werewolf charged with transgressing against the Garou as a whole (and thus against Gaia) comes before the Council of Elders. The accused need not actually be present at the trial, but absence is almost always seen as an admission of guilt. Usually, the entire Council convenes for truly staggering transgressions against the Litany. Otherwise, only a few members of the Council need be present to act as judges. The exact form the trial takes varies with the sept itself. In multiple-tribe septs, the judging format usually follows from the tribe composing the sept's majority.

Although each tribe has its own format for judging breaches against Garou and Gaia, all proceedings take, at most, a matter of days to resolve. The typical case is judged in a few hours, if that. The werewolf who violates the Litany or the laws of their sept or tribe can usually expect to face one of four punishments: shaming, shunning, exile, or death.

• **Shaming** is the punishment of choice for those who have let their pride, cowardice or self-absorption lead them to sins of negligence. Punishment rites such as the Stone of Scorn, the Voice of the Jackal or the Satire Rite are common examples of shaming. Werewolves being the proud creatures that they are, this tactic is perhaps more effective than it would be in human society.

• **Shunning** is the next step in severity, applicable to those who placed fellow Garou or others necessary to Gaia at unnecessary risk or to those who have failed to mend their ways after previous punishments. The Rite of Ostracism is the method of choice. The shunning (during which no other Garou will even acknowledge the target's existence) can last from a week to a lunar year, although the transgressor isn't told the actual duration. Sometimes a shunning will last until the transgressor truly mends her ways (although, again, she isn't told that this is how her punishment will end).

• **Exile** is given to a werewolf whose betrayal of his duty was unforgivable, but who is considered insufficiently dangerous or corrupt to kill outright. The permanent form of the Rite of Ostracism completes this process; from that point on, the Garou is considered Ronin, without sept, pack or tribe. For pack creatures like werewolves, this is a harsh punishment indeed.

• **Death** is the ultimate punishment. If the offender's crimes are so horrible as to mandate a sentence of death, but the offender herself is considered to still have a vestige of honor, she is the subject of the Rite of the Hunt. If, however, she has openly betrayed her own kind to the Wyrm or otherwise erased any lingering honor she once had, then her final fate is Gaia's Vengeful Teeth. Those who die in such a fashion are considered less than Garou — honorless, valueless creatures unfit to walk Gaia even as Ronin.

Tribal Tradition and the Litany

No matter what a Philodox may say, the Litany is seldom absolute. Most tribes put their own spin on the Litany's laws, enforcing crimes against the Litany a little more…selectively. For example, a Silver Fang who butchers humans indiscriminately will be tried fairly severely for violating the tenet "Respect Those Beneath Ye — All Are of Gaia." A Red Talon who does the same, though…well, his elders might turn a blind eye, or claim that the young hothead in question was following his duty to "Combat the Wyrm Wherever It Dwells and Whenever It Breeds." The Talons have long believed that the Wyrm breeds in the hearts of humans, after all, and it's hard to actually *disprove* that….

However, a sept must uphold a common standard of justice. If the aforementioned Red Talon were charged with violating the Litany in a multitribal sept, his elders would be able to do little for him; the sept's laws follow the majority opinion, not the extreme. Those who break the Litany in tribally "condoned" (or, rather, ignored) fashion must be careful to do so out of the sight of members of less understanding tribes.

LYCANTHROPE

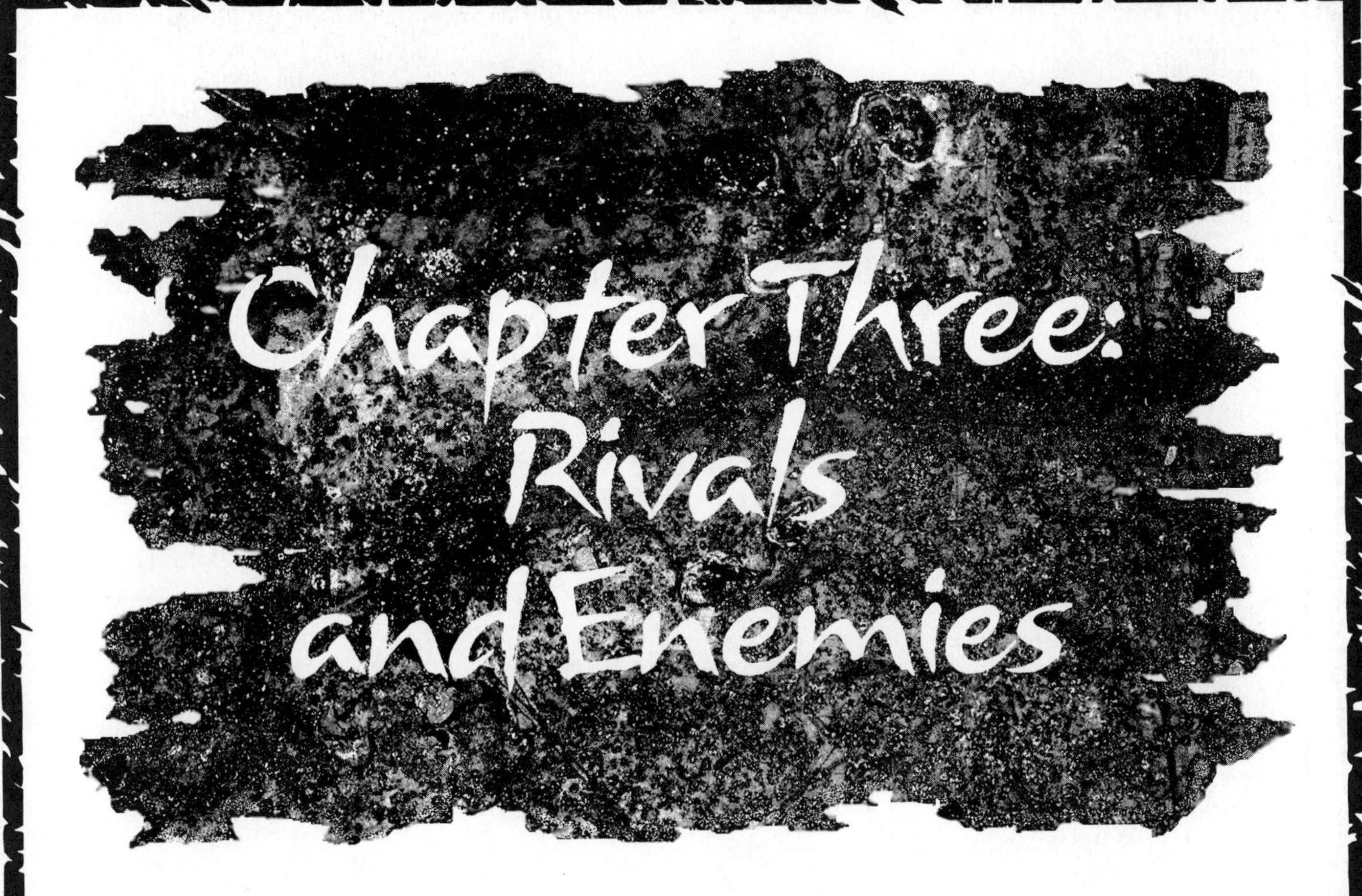

The Garou aren't alone in the World of Darkness. There are a number of other supernatural creatures that prowl the cities and wild places, pursuing their own agendas. The werewolves have crossed paths with them now and again, and pass on the knowledge they've gained from such encounters to their allies.

The question is, how much do werewolves know? Sure, your players can go pick up a copy of **Vampire: The Masquerade** and be quoting clan names and Discipline effects within the hour. Werewolves in the World of Darkness don't have that luxury. Their information is limited; it's just not possible for a werewolf to go slumming in a vampire hangout and pick up the lingo by eavesdropping. And they certainly don't go freely exchanging information with mages or vampires or the like; they tried that a few times, and the end result was always the same — fallen caerns and dead Garou. In the World of Darkness, only a fool trusts an outsider to be exactly what they say they are. They might be telling the truth — but more often, they're not.

Hence this chapter. Although the **Werewolf: The Apocalypse** rulebook offers some basic, hard-and-fast information about vampires, mages and the like, that's not very helpful when it comes time to determine just how well-educated the local werewolves are in such matters.

The following information is told from the perspective of the werewolves themselves, in particular the werewolves that have made a habit of studying each supernatural group in question. In addition, sidebars sum up the quick version of what *most* werewolves know about the given group. Generally speaking, assume that most Garou that the characters meet know the information in the sidebars, whereas a mentor or elder who specializes in the lore of the given supernatural creature may have access to the larger body of lore.

And, of course, remember that not everything the werewolves believe is true…

Vampires

As recounted by Buries-the-Dead, Silent Strider Ahroun:

I have heard it said that a people is defined by its enemies. We know this to be true of the Garou, for we have many, many foes that wish us dead — and we are forced to become warriors in response. Know this, though, young one: Of all the monsters that you will be forced to oppose in this world, there are perhaps none more wretched and intolerable than the Leeches, the dead who walk, the Cadavers — yes, vampires.

Listen to me, now. You will hear it said that not all vampires are wholly and maliciously evil. You will learn that a few werewolves, particularly among the Glass Walkers and Shadow Lords, feel that it is better to strike truce with the undead than to waste lives warring on them. You will hear that vampires are sometimes victims, creatures who did not ask to have their souls rent from them and their bellies filled with hunger for blood.

This is all true. But you do yourself, your pack, your tribe, and your Mother wrong if ever you *trust* one of the undead.

The Leeches are creatures made of lies. They lie to snare their prey; they lie to hide their lairs; they lie because they have forgotten how to tell the truth. Even those who did not ask for their fate will do whatever they must to preserve their half-existences; even the most meek and reclusive vampire would rather kill in order to survive another night than simply die. They frenzy, as we do; anything that might endanger them, such as fire or the rising sun, will drive them berserk. They do not have the power to overcome their condition, and they do not have the will to renounce their undead existence at all costs. A very few boast no greater sin than the weak will that prevents them from resisting the urge to harm others. These few may not properly *deserve* to die — but they *must*. Their souls are gone to wherever human spirits go; what remains is a shell filled with Wyrm-given hunger that remembers vaguely how a human should act. Pray for the soul that has fled, even as you release what remains from the body.

Listen. All vampires have the potential for supernatural strength, speed and endurance; not one of them is weak as the person it once was. The more recently they have fed, the stronger they are — blood is not merely an addiction to them, it is the source of their power. Age also strengthens them; the corruption in their bodies grows over time, granting them more and more power as they grow older and older. Would that evil would consume itself more quickly — but if that were true, there would be no need for us.

I have hunted — and studied — the vampires for a long time. They seem to be social creatures, but their society is a cruel one. Whether subtle or overt, they enjoy exercising cruelties on humans, "playing with their food," as it were. Their mortal lineage seems to be important to them; I have marked a few who spoke openly of families and bloodlines. Though I cannot see how a corpse can pretend to pure breeding, the illusion is apparently quite important to the Leeches.

I have marked four different castes among them, not unlike the castes of other human societies. A caste seems to influence a vampire's particular strengths; I cannot say whether this is a learned thing or if the vampires are "born" to their abilities. Ultimately, though, it makes little difference whether aptitude determines caste or caste determines aptitude. No caste is any less monstrous than the others, no matter how civilized they may seem.

The Deformed

It is hard to mistake one of the Deformed for any other caste. Their corruption is made manifest on their faces, in ways oddly appropriate to the nature of their hungers. The Deformed caste is the lowest among the vampire hierarchy; even other Leeches shun their obvious debasement. In return, the Deformed appear to devote their energies to "sharing" their taints and afflictions with humanity.

Some are scarred and twisted, even half-melted like lepers; it is my belief that these are disease-spreaders, who pass blood-borne diseases from human to human. Some appear to be rotting corpses, as though the power of the blood they drink is no longer capable of staving off decomposition. Such putrefied creatures wield the power of unnatural death and decay; it is their talent to wither and shrivel the young and vital before its time. A few are even deformed in the manner of animals, with patches of fur and strange deformities like undead parodies of the fictional Dr. Moreau's creations. These creatures spread madness and bloodlust.

Although the Deformed are easy to recognize in their true forms, know that these beasts have learned the art of illusion, all the better to conceal their deformities from their prey. They have exceptionally keen senses, and some mimic the powers of animals. Though I think they are too ignorant to realize that they insult the natural order by aping the strengths of living things, that makes the insult no easier to bear.

The Warriors

The next highest caste is that of the Warriors; or perhaps they are a caste of commoners instead. It would seem that this caste is by far the most populous of all. I call them Warriors because they are most likely to focus on the physical aspects of their power — strength, speed, heightened senses, and even clever tricks such as invisibility. I do not mean to imply that they share a common martial discipline; they do not. Instead, they are the infantry of the Leeches' regime, all too often awkwardly thrown together like a primitive militia.

But this militia has fangs! As I said, they are creatures of great physical prowess and they often learn (or are created with? I cannot say) other, more subtle powers. I theorize that perhaps the higher castes are given to recruiting their new kind from the Warrior caste now and again, and the common vampires you face who wield atypically versatile powers are apprentices-in-training to those above them.

The Warriors are numerous, and that is their greatest strength. However, they only rarely know the tricks of traveling in packs. If you catch them alone, they are easy prey — I have heard no tales of a Warrior that has achieved the might of old age.

The Warlocks

The vampires that use sorcery to achieve their ends are perhaps the rarest of all — and not to be underestimated. I do not believe them to be the highest among the castes; they seem to serve the role of vizier to their superiors. They are extremely dangerous, however — in my experience, the very worst of all.

The magic of the witch-caste comes from no good source. It does not rely on the spirit world as directly as do our rites; not even Banes answer the call of an undead sorcerer. It may be a blend of their blood-power, human magic and Wyrm-granted investments. I believe, personally, that it derives from the Dark Umbra and the things within — or perhaps even the Abyss. I have never dared pry too far; even the Uktena know that there are some secrets that must not be learned, lest they nest in your brain like a spider and drive you to madness.

Never — and I say *never* — underestimate the power of an undead witch's magic. It was a great cabal of these monsters that drove my people from their homeland, setting ghosts on our heels and cursing us to wander forevermore. I do not know what spirits, living or dead, they drew on to harness such power; I am thankful they have not used such power since.

Of all the vampire castes, no greater enemy will you find than these witches, creatures of the red desert and worshippers of the Night itself. Tread most carefully when you find one; never let it capture your hair, nails or blood. Do not enter its sanctum unprepared. And if you find the opportunity to destroy it, do so without hesitation.

The Nobility

The most beautiful and strongest-willed among the vampires naturally rise to positions of prominence among their kind. The popular "romantic" notion of vampires among humans — does it not seem galling, that humans would idolize the human-seeming monsters that prey upon them and demonize animal predators that walk on four legs, or swim in the sea? — finds some truth here. Many of the ruling Leech caste are inhumanly beautiful — those that are not have tricks of their own.

What Most Garou Know: Vampires

- Vampires stink of the Wyrm; they are also redolent of Weaver energies, although not as strongly.
- Vampires must feed on human or animal blood to survive. They are not honorable hunters, however, and hunt as if it were sport to them.
- Vampires fear the sun, and are harmed by its rays. Fire will also destroy vampires. This would seem to indicate that purity is anathema to them.
- Vampires thrive in the cities, and will do all in their power to expand the cities as far as they can.
- Vampires can exist ("living" is not a good word for what they do) for centuries; they may even be functionally immortal.
- And, of course, homids may "know" whatever they've seen in movies about vampires; most Garou, however, know better than to trust Hollywood's reservoir of occult lore.

You see, the ruling caste is the one with the greatest power to control the minds of others. That would seem to be common sense, after all. And they have many, many ways of exerting their power. Of course, some may transfix you with their gaze. Others can control anyone who has ever been tricked into drinking their blood. Still others use ritual spells and hypnotic songs.

Yes, spells; it is worth mentioning that the ruling caste seems to be able to access the powers of any of the castes below them. They might possess superior strength, or the ability to mask themselves under illusion, or forbidden rituals calling on the Wyrm. It is my belief that they can compel those of other castes to teach them such tricks, whether by right of their noble status or by using their mind-raping powers. They are even all the more terrifying when you consider that these same powers grant them great power and influence in the mortal world; they might have politicians, policemen, bankers or even generals under their thumbs. Thankfully, the ruling caste is the rarest, and many of its members seem to spend an inordinate amount of time attempting to wrest power from one another. They are dangerous, dangerous enemies, everything that we fear about the Leeches.

Pardon me — does it seem unusual for an Ahroun such as myself to use the word "fear"? Perhaps you are right. But it is good to fear the vampires, for they are an ancient and wily enemy. Were they any weaker, we would have destroyed them by now — and yet they thrive all the same. You would do well to keep a healthy respect, even a small amount of fear for the Leeches and their powers. Respect them — and by respecting them, you will learn never to underestimate their ability to seduce, deceive and destroy whenever it suits them to do so. In knowing them for what they are, you gain the power to fight them, as you must.

Mages

From the teachings of Ingrid St. Joan, Black Fury Strega:

The Galliards will tell you that the witches are our enemies. That is because there are many instances in the past where a caern came under attack, and only afterwards did we learn that it was not the forces of the Wyrm — but rather, greedy warlocks who came to drink the caern's energies. And they do not know restraint; a caern will dry up and die before a cabal of warlocks realizes that they should stop drinking its power. My sisters have told you that I have conversed, even fought beside shamans and witches of noble enough purpose before — this is true. But never would I let them across the bawn of my caern, nor even would I tell them why. If even *one* succumbed to a desperate thirst for Gnosis, and came stealing to the caern in hopes of filching a few sips of the caern's energy — I would have been guilty of violating one of the Litany's most sacred laws and my life would have been rightfully forfeit.

But yes, I have cooperated with them — always conditionally, but I have done so. Not all are dire enemies; they are all dangerous, and often bad to know, but not all are enemies. I take it you would like to know more?

There is a great difference, you see, between a sorcerer and a shaman — or to put it another way, between a witch and a Wise One. Many human peoples note the difference between one who uses magic or medicine only to heal and soothe, and one who uses her...gifts to serve her own ends, or even to harm others. The first is a shaman — the second, a sorcerer. Most mages, I fear, are the latter.

As the legends go, magi are not entitled to the powers they wield — they use forbidden knowledge to achieve their ends. You see, these warlocks are able to rewrite the natural order, if you will — they do not draw their powers from the spirits as we do, but rather force the world to obey their will for a short period of time. Where an Uktena might call on the power loaned to her by Bluejay to emulate the jay's flight, a warlock will force gravity to repel him rather than draw him closer to the earth's bosom. Where I would speak the tongue of spirits taught to me by my spirit friends, a witch would use her power to compel spirits to speak in a language she understands.

I can't say for certain if their power is stolen or forbidden, but it is true that warlocks are punished if they go too far or dare too much. What punishes them? Why, the world itself, it would seem — or their own magic. I've seen a witch devoured by the forces she tried to call on. It wasn't a pleasant sight, although it was...somehow appropriate. The strike was so swift, I didn't have time to catch its scent — its true scent, if you will. Even now, I don't know whether it was Gaia's will, the Weaver's power or even the magic itself that decided to write the witch out of existence.

The most obvious explanation is the most popular among our kind. A warlock's power, strange as it is, ravages the very face of Nature itself. It leaves furrows in the flesh of Gaia — no, not the earth, but rather all of the world. A warlock who forces the wind to carry him leaves invisible scars in the air itself. These gouges rapidly heal, but would they not be a constant irritation to the Mother, like a dust mote in Her eye? The reprisals, when they come, seem random; but to a fly struck by a horse's tail or a mosquito absently smashed by a human hand, their fate must seem random, too. Does the mosquito understand that its bite is in some small way debilitating or undesirable to the vast mountain it feeds from? No. And neither do the warlocks understand that their powers are offensive to the Mother. Just as the mosquito looks at the vastness of a person and sees only a meal, the warlock looks at the world and sees only that which he desires.

However...there is another possibility. Perhaps the reprisals visited on these witches are not sent by a sleeping Gaia, but rather by the Weaver. As you know, the Weaver is not fond of...variables. Everything must obey her laws, or else it is not permitted to exist. I know this is her command; I have the scars that mark her displeasure with my guardianship of the Wyld. How furious the witches must make her — even we Garou obey the laws of the universe ordained by Gaia. The witches don't do even that. So the Weaver lashes out at these poor fools, smashing them when they go too far, forcing them to obey the natural order. She may be right in doing so — but it is hard to say whether that is one of the few good instincts remaining to her, or whether it is another symptom of her madness.

I wonder at the truth of this. It may be that the truth is a blend of both explanations; perhaps the warlocks' power pains and irritates the Mother, and the Weaver watches for the Mother to flinch, knowing that the source of the irritation is her enemy as well. It's not for me to say.

You will know a witch by her reliance on human magical traditions. As I understand it, the power is not in the trappings they use — be they books of "Egyptian" spells, voudoun rituals, shamanic dances, Crowley-inspired Satanic incantations or what have you — but in the magi themselves. Unlike our own rites, which are empowered by the spirits, their rituals seem to lend them a sort of focus, a framework to channel their energy. I can't say why it is that some use numerology and alchemy and others rely on meditative techniques — the foibles of their peculiar mindsets, I suppose. One witch in particular protested that there is a secret conspiracy of mages who disguise their magic as technology, but I believe her to have been mentally unsound; she seemed out of sorts with the modern age, and may not have been able to deal with the idea that technology can accomplish things formerly believed to be in the province of magic alone.

I mention that their patterns of thought are unusual, yes. Many magi have a deeply rooted need to believe in something, no matter how peculiar. They may draw comfort from their belief in a patriarchal god, or they may believe most sincerely that their actions of mental assault and seduction are not only condonable, but also necessary. They are obsessive creatures, driven by the need to overcome the flaws of their mortal shells — for all a warlock's power, his body is still as frail as any man's — and the desire to see their will made manifest on the world. This makes them exceptionally dangerous, for you can never tell what convictions a witch may hide from you, convictions that rule her soul.

And yes, those convictions may be dedicated to the Wyrm. There are witches who practice the blackest forms of magic, who have fallen to the Enemy. These are the worst sorts — they knowingly consort with Banes and fomori, and have sold their souls to whatever Malfean entity has chosen to present itself to them. They are insidious sorts, subtle and decadent, and they cannot be tolerated to live. Are there mages who follow the Weaver or Wyld, by compare? I cannot

What Most Garou Know: Mages

- Mages possess the power to somehow rewrite the laws of nature; they are capable of performing great miracles or hideous atrocities given enough time and effort.
- Mages are not meant to possess their powers — or at the very least, to use them as they do. Their powers offend Gaia or the Weaver, who punish them for their hubris from time to time.
- Mages feed on Gnosis, and there are many tales of them mounting raids on caerns to drink the sacred places dry of the Mother's lifeblood.
- Mages learn magic according to human tradition; their powers run the gamut from Satanic-style ritualism to New Age pseudo-shamanism to Taoist alchemy.
- Mages can and do fall to the Wyrm. They do not seem inclined to offer themselves to the Weaver or Wyld.
- There are a few mages who practice much greater restraint, either to avoid the spirits' retribution or out of genuine reverence for the way the world works. These mages are not always enemies, although many are still opposed to the Gaian ideal.

say. I think there must be, but I've never heard of any who fit that description.

A witch will probably be your enemy. She may be a temporary ally. She may indeed seem worthy to be a friend. But I caution you — do not stand too close. She exercises powers she was not meant to use, probably with the full knowledge that she runs the risk of being punished by the universe for her temerity. Whether you agree that she has the right to use her powers or not, it is dangerous to stand too close to her — and by calling her friend, you also are in danger of making her enemies your own. If the stories are true, and the witches are anathema to Gaia Herself — then may heaven help you, for your own kind never will.

Hunters

From the favorite rant of Trash-80, Bone Gnawer Ragabash:

Look. You know there's always going to be some human who can fight back. The Veil ain't perfect, and now and again some guy with solid brass testicles finds the courage to stare one of us in the eye before he unloads two barrels of silver buck into our chest. 'Course, he ain't long for the world after that, 'cause the human ain't been born who's a match for one of us — particularly an angry packmate — without some powerful mojo on his side.

'Least, that's the way it used to be. Things are different now, since the Red Star showed up and all.

You haven't heard about these guys. Trust me. They don't get out in the boonies much — they crop up in places where there's a lot of humans to give rise to 'em and a lot of monsters to go huntin'. And that means cities. But what we're dealing with here is a whole new breed of brass monkey, something that ain't quite a wizard and ain't quite a mortal. The kicker is, they're able to see us — and vampires, and fomori, and Gaia knows what else — for what we are, no matter how well we're disguised.

And it gets better. These guys have some kinda supernatural power juicing them up, something that ain't quite Umbral. It's versatile stuff; it makes a butter knife as deadly as a klaive, or gives 'em the ability to look a vampire in the eye without getting hypmotized. Crazy shit, man, and no two have the same power. Only I think that "seeing monsters" thing works for them no matter what.

I've heard a few stories about who's been giving these guys their powers, and why. I'll tell you right out that the theory that they're being fueled by the spirits of the cities themselves is bunk — I asked Momma Tampa myself if that was so, and she ain't the sort to lie to a guy like me. Some folks say they've been empowered by the Wyrm — or, depending on who you believe, the Weaver — to hunt down anyone and everything that might be a potential threat to their Celestine. Of course, they don't smell much like Wyrm or Weaver, 'cept on an individual basis, so that theory kind of sucks, if you ask me. I've also heard that they were empowered by the Wyrm in some last desperate flash of sanity, sent out to restore Balance to the world. It's a better theory, but again, they don't smell like the Wyrm — and what's balancing about genocide, anyway? I even hear that they're something like the magi — maybe they're the next evolutionary step up from humanity, kind of a humanity-with-the-power-to-defend-itself, if you know what I mean. And they do tend to crop up in the cities, so maybe that's accurate — maybe the big ol' collective spirit of humanity finally got around to providing someone to fight against the Impergium, only they're about a zillion years too late.

But who knows? *They* don't. They don't have a clue, man. Poor bastards, the only thing they know is that they woke up and started seeing monsters everywhere and they've held on just long enough to find out that it's no hallucination. And since they're just ordinary folks at heart, that means they see the need to watch out for their kids, or to clean up their neighborhoods, or whatever. So they go vigilante — and they're just tough enough to be dangerous.

I dunno what this means in the long run. I don't think they run in packs big enough to be a threat to any caern, but who knows? The Apocalypse is on us, man. Maybe this is the Eighth Sign or something. Humanity's fighting back, even against those of us who think humans are worth keeping around. Keep an eye out, that's all I'm saying. And spread the word. We could be onto something huge here.

What Most Garou Know: Hunters

As far as most werewolves are concerned, most humans who take up hunting werewolves are simply ordinary people with the willpower to resist the Delirium and the idiocy to think they're a match for Garou. Most Garou don't even know that the "imbued" class of hunter is even out there; even those who encounter an Imbued face-to-face are unlikely to be able to tell the hunter apart from a subtle fomor, mage or otherwise enhanced human.

The Restless Dead

From a concolation address by Solomon Scarwound of the Ivory Priesthood:

None of you would disagree that the undead have no place in this world. They do have a place in Gaia's creation, that much is true — and that place is the Dark Umbra. None of us should begrudge a human's spirit the right to walk in the place prepared for it should it be unwilling or unable to pass further on. And yet, the Dark Umbra itself has seen the battle fires of the Apocalypse, and the ramifications are many and troubling.

The Eye of the Wyrm has appeared even in the skies of the Dark Umbra. It is faint there, but its color is unmistakable — *color*, in a land where all else is black and gray. When it tore its way into the Dark Umbra, the force of its entry whipped up countless storms, tempests that wrack the land of the dead from one end to the other. I have heard it said that the very cities of the dead themselves are in ruin, flooded beneath the dark waters raised by these storms.

We should not be surprised, then, that the ghosts have decided to flee their world for a safer one. But that "safer" world is the physical realm!

We already knew that ghosts would manifest themselves in the physical world from time to time. This was always a great effort for them, and not without cost. Only the most dire need could drive a ghost that far — a need for vengeance, or a desire to see a loved one through a tragedy, or whatever goal kept them from leaving their former lives behind. Now, however, the wall between the Dark Umbra and this world has been weakened by the storms, and the ghosts are finding it easier — or perhaps they are simply just that much more desperate — to cross over.

Many of them are even now taking refuge in their old bodies, animating their cold corpses with nothing more than the pure strength of will. The tales of battles with these revenants have increased sevenfold in the last year. The Wyrm rides some of these creatures, but not all. Not all draw strength from the spirits of corruption. Indeed, their former lives seem to provide them with strength — my fellow priests and I have seen ghosts and revenants that grew stronger the closer they drew to completing their goals.

This strength floods them in many ways. Those who wear bodies suffer none of the weaknesses of flesh — they require no blood, no air, not even the presence

of their internal organs. However, much of their strength seems to be devoted to their vessels, and so they are unable to call on many of the powers of their disembodied brethren. Yes, the incorporeal undead can affect the physical; they can move things, change the weather, even take temporary physical form. Some can even touch our very spirits, draining our strength to feed their own.

How do we fight them? Not easily. Even if we find ways into the Dark Umbra, they are no less powerful there. Many, in fact, are far stronger in their homeland. They seem to have difficulty penetrating the Gauntlet, at least those without bodies — but then again, the cities are cesspools of the violence and anguish that breeds ghosts, and I cannot say that the Gauntlet is foolproof. Indeed, the surest way to fight a ghost may be to help it achieve its goals — without the tether of desire holding it to this plane, it has little choice but to pass on beyond.

I realize that this may seem a small concern, with the Leeches teeming like flies on carrion and the armies of the Enemy marshalling for their final attack. Nonetheless, my noble friends, I suggest that you remain wary. We make many ghosts when we go to war. Some of those are sure to remember us.

What Most Garou Know: Wraiths

• Wraiths are the spirits of dead humans who are somehow prevented from passing on to their final reward (or reincarnation, or being reunited with Gaia) and are marooned in the Dark Umbra.

• Wraiths linger on because of some tragedy that makes them unable to rest.

• Wraiths are often subject to Wyrm-taint, but are not intrinsically tainted. Their taint usually comes from succumbing to dark emotions such as regret or anger.

• Wraiths are not spirits, and cannot be dealt with in such a fashion.

What Most Garou Know: Walking Dead

Most werewolves aren't familiar with animated corpses as enemies; the numbers of the Walking Dead have never been particularly impressive until recently. Apart from a general knowledge that these zombies seem to be tied to the Red Star, and that they exist, the Walking Dead are considered to fill much the same niche as wraiths.

Faeries

As told by Ceridwen Hunting Horn, Fianna Galliard

Sweet Mother, you're asking me *now* about the Fair Folk? Why not ask twenty years ago, fifty, a hundred? No, that's not fair and I know it — but it's a little late to be taking an interest in them. Their glory days are long gone.

They're still around, yes. That much is true. But they're a pale shadow of what they used to be. The fae of today, compared with their forebears — they're like our Kinfolk compared to us. Back so long ago, there wasn't anything human in them at all — now they're more like changelings, fae babes raised by humans who have taken on more than a little mortal blood.

It's sad, but what they need to keep going is mortal belief. Look at us — our traditions have endured in spite of the mortal world. The faeries, though, they need people to believe in the romance of the medieval world, to dream tales of fae as they used to be. Their legend hasn't changed with the times, and unlike us, they can't rely on their own strength to see them through.

I heard tell that they're creatures of the Wyld, like us. It may be so. The Weaver hurts them bad, that's for sure. We can't exactly recognize just where their spirit portion comes from, but it can't flourish in areas where the Gauntlet's high and nobody has need of fairytales.

They can be nasty, and dangerous. There are goblins among them, horrible creatures that'd gnaw the flesh from your bones if they thought they could get away with it. But I tell you, you've never seen beauty like that of one of their nobles. Even the faded, pale, half-human ones are still unearthly, creatures that could almost make you believe in a finer world than this one.

I heard tell that some of them fall in love with some of us, and I'll tell you that's something to be avoided. They think nothing of throwing a glamour over your eyes and charming you into falling in love with them, because the wretched creatures just can't stand to hear the word "no." A talisman of iron is usually the charm you need to resist their powers; if you need to drive them away without actually killing them, you can press it against their flesh and they'll leave you be.

Faeries. I tell you, if there's a world left when the war is over, and the forests start growing thick and full again, and there are more humans who have fallen in love with the world than those who haven't — maybe then you'll see one. But I think instead the last of them

What Most Garou Know: Faeries

• Faeries are, if not actually extinct, so rare that they are nearly gone.

• Faeries are allergic to the Weaver, and suffer in areas where she is strong.

• A faerie's powers generally have to do with illusion and bewitchment; they aren't powerful warriors.

will die before the last of us does — which might not be that far off.

Pentex

From an email sent by Third Shift, Glass Walker Ragabash:

It's worse than we thought. I just got word from Detroit, and they verified all we knew and added some details. Hence the encryption. This is big-league stuff.

• First off, the name is definitely "Pentex." Big-ass multinational megacorp, holdings all over the place. Seems to have once been an oil company that diversified; doesn't produce anything itself these days, but leaves that to the subsids.

• Endron Oil, Magadon (the pharmaceut bunch), Ardus (those waste-disposal jerks) and Rainbow Inc. (the plastics people) are definitely all tied together. They're all subsidiaries of this Pentex bitch.

• Each one of those guys has black-ops-level stuff brewing in plants here and there. We're talking poisons, drugs, that kind of thing. These deep black plants are utterly deniable, and loaded with security — including Banes and fomori. You heard me.

• Said ties with Wyrm-spirits and BSDs [shit, man! I hadn't even guessed!] seem to imply that the top echelon is somehow tied in with the Wyrm, and are working according to some agenda thereof. Possible Maeljin Incarna influence here. Seems to be top echelon only; most employees seem to be ordinary corporate bastards, no worse than the usual.

• The lax pollution standards seem to virtually be regulation. Again, M.I. influence?

• Black ops teams — commandos, assassins, and the like — are definitely at their disposal. Completely deniable mercs. Rumor has it they're immune to the Veil, and are trained to fight werewolves(!), even to the point of packing silver ammo.

• Other confirmed subsidiaries: Avalon Inc. [toys]; Circinus Brands [RJR's main competitor to-

bacco-wise]; Good House [paper products; serious bad-practice loggers]; Hallahan Fishing [number three on Greenpeace's hit list]; Herculean [firearms]; Herrick's [yeah, the grocery store chain]; King Breweries [dumping some of that shit out of my fridge as soon as I send this]; Nastrum [*major* military manufacturer I'd been looking at]; OmniTV [I shit you not]; O'Tolley's [which isn't a surprise to anyone who's ever eaten there]; Tellus [videogames, of which I've got like half their fall lineup]; and Vesuvius [the publishers, in deep w/Good House].

• Agenda uncertain, but we've all but verified (a) making a buck as fast as possible and fuck ethics and (b) help turn the buying public into brain-dead consuming machines. We're still not sure about (c) fuck the planet over and make everyone as miserable as possible so that the Masters get that much stronger, have a much easier job taking over, and set us up real nice — but right now, it seems plausible to *me*.

By damn, we'd better disseminate this to the elders outside the city limits, ASAP. Sure, they're gonna be skeptical, but I don't care. *Make* them listen to you; this isn't the time for vital information to be lost in a pile of mistrust for "urrah." I don't know how we can fight something this big, but I tell ya, we gotta try.

What Most Garou Know: Pentex

• Werewolves who haven't made it a habit to keep up with the corporate world (which includes *many* elders) are unlikely to even know that there's such a thing as "Pentex"; its logo isn't present on the factories and trucks that do its dirty work, and only the highest-ranking employees of its subsidiaries are in the habit of mentioning its name fairly regularly.

• Most werewolves involved in the fight against corporate abuse of the land (and people) are aware of some of the "problem" subsidiaries like Magadon and Endron, the ones who seem to have some access to Banes and fomori. Some of these werewolves know about the "higher power" of Pentex, and some don't.

PENTEX

Expanded Renown Rules

The Renown guidelines given in the main rulebook for **Werewolf: The Apocalypse** are fairly loose, and intentionally so. For one, loose guidelines place more control in the hands of the Storyteller — a comprehensive list of near-everything that could possibly affect Renown leads to added bookkeeping, as well as setting one general rate for Renown gain. A looser structure encourages the Storyteller to tailor the rate of rank gain to her own tastes, either granting more Renown than a detailed chart might suggest in order to speed advancement to high Rank, or granting fewer than suggested in order to keep advancement more hard-won. More importantly — and it's a shame to have to say this — loose guidelines discourage unscrupulous players from paging through the Renown charts and tailoring their characters' actions for maximum Renown gain rather than simply roleplaying their characters, right or wrong.

Even so, you may find the following chart of sample Renown awards somewhat helpful when it comes time to adjudicating just what is or isn't worthy of reward (or punishment). Again, this isn't meant to be comprehensive — it's only a number of examples of behavior that deserves Renown modifications. We encourage Storytellers to create whatever awards (or penalties) seem appropriate to the deeds of the characters, or even to fudge them from day to day; as long as you remain largely consistent and even-handed, nobody should complain.

Sample Renown Awards

Activity	Glory	Honor	Wisdom
Combat and Encounters			
Besting someone (including a spirit) in a riddle contest	0	0	3
Showing restraint in the face of certain death	0	1	3
Ending a threat without serious harm to any Garou	0	0	5
Surviving an Incapacitating wound	2	0	0
Surviving any toxic waste attack	2	0	0
Attacking a much more powerful force without aid	0	0	-3
Attacking a minion of the Wyrm without regard to personal safety	3	0	0
Defeating a formidable supernatural threat not of the Wyrm (strand spider, master mage, fae warrior, Fera)	2	0	0
Defeating a very powerful supernatural threat not of the Wyrm (archmage, fae sorcerer)	3	0	0
Defeating a minor Wyrm threat (Kalus, a Bane-infested animal, young vampires)	2	0	0
Defeating a average Wyrm threat (Blight Child, fomori)	3	0	0
Defeating a strong Wyrm threat (Psychomachiae, Black Spiral Dancer pack)	5	0	0
Defeating a very powerful Wyrm threat (Nexus Crawler, elder vampires)	7	0	0
...permanently destroying/killing the threat in question	+1	0	0
...without a single other Garou being hurt	+1	0	0
...without being hurt or damaged in the process	+1	0	0
...and the threat(s) were armed with silver weapons	+1	0	0
Detecting the Wyrm			
Revealing, with certain proof, that a human or Kinfolk is "of the Wyrm"	0	0	2
Falsely accusing a Kinfolk of being "of the Wyrm"	0	-2	-3
Revealing, with certain proof, that an area or object is "of the Wyrm"	0	0	3
Revealing, with certain proof, that a Garou is "of the Wyrm"	0	0	6
Falsely accusing a Garou of being "of the Wyrm"	0	-5	-4
Mystical			
Purifying a Wyrm-tainted object, person, or place	0	0	2
Summoning an Incarna avatar	0	0	2
Traveling to any of the Umbral Realms and surviving	3	0	0
Successfully completing a spirit quest in the Umbra	0	0	3
Failing to succeed in a spirit quest in the Umbra	0	0	-3
Having and properly following a prophetic dream	0	0	5
Giving a prophetic warning that later comes true	0	0	5
Ignoring omens, dreams and the like for no good reason (i.e., they may be of the Wyrm)	0	0	-3
Binding "inappropriate" items to oneself through the Rite of Talisman Dedication (such as chainsaws, pagers, or wristwatches). This does not apply to Glass Walkers or Bone Gnawers	0	0	-2
Spending a year in ritualistic seclusion (fasting, mediation, etc.)	0	0	5
After following mystic signs and advice...			
Discovering a talen	0	0	1
Discovering a fetish	0	0	2

Activity	Glory	Honor	Wisdom
Discovering ancient Garou lore	0	0	3
Discovering a Pathstone (see *Rite of the Opened Bridge*, **Werewolf**, pg. 158)	0	0	4
Discovering an ancient caern that was lost	0	0	7
Rites and Gifts:			
Performing a Moot Rite	0	2	0
Refusing to perform a Moot Rite when asked	0	-3	0
Missing a Moot Rite	0	0	-1
Performing a Rite of Passage	0	2	1
Receiving a Rite of Wounding	2	0	0
Performing a Rite of Caern Building	3	5	7
Participating in a Rite of Caern Building	5	3	
Participation in a successful Great Hunt rite	3	0	0
Participation in a failed Great Hunt rite	-2	0	0
Suffering the Rite of Ostracism	-1	-7	-1
Suffering the Stone of Scorn	0	-8	-2
Suffering the Rite of the Jackal	-2	-7	0
Suffering a Satire Rite	lose one Rank level and all temporary Renown		
Performing a Punishment Rite	0	2	0
Performing a Punishment Rite unjustly (botching the rite roll)	0	-5	0
Refusing to participate in a rite	0	0	-1
Giggling, joking, or otherwise being disrespectful during a rite (depends on the severity)	0	0	-1 to -5
Learning a new rite	0	0	1
Discovering/creating a new rite	0	0	5
Discovering/creating a new Gift	0	0	7
Fetishes:			
Creating a talen	0	0	1
Using a fetish for the good of the sept or tribe	0	0	2
Using a fetish for selfish reasons only	0	0	-1
Creating a fetish	0	0	4
Owning a klaive (awarded once, only after three moons of use)	2	1	0
Owning a grand klaive (awarded once, only after three moons of use)	3	2	0
Sacrificing a fetish for the good of the sept or tribe	0	0	4
Accidentally breaking a fetish or talen	0	0	-1 to -5
Accidentally breaking or losing a klaive	0	-3	0
Caern Activities			
Helping guard a caern	0	1	0
Staying at your post when on caern watch, even when tempted not to	0	2	1
Not staying at your post when on watch	0	-3	0
Not helping guard a caern, even when asked to	0	-3	0
Keeping a caern safe from humans through trickery or negotiation	0	0	4
Helping to prevent a caern from being overrun by the Wyrm	3	4	0
Not preventing a caern from being overrun by the Wyrm	-3	-7	0
Died while defending a caern (posthumous)	5	8	
Single-handedly prevented a caern from being taken by the Wyrm	5	8	0

Activity	Glory	Honor	Wisdom
Garou Relations and Society			
Teaching other Garou (depends on the depth of study)	0	1 to 5	3 to 5
Learning the Silver Record, completely (a lifetime's work)	0	7	8
For a homid Garou, surviving to age 75	0	8	10
For a lupus Garou, surviving to age 65	0	8	10
Breed:			
For a homid, ignoring one's wolf nature for too long	0	0	-3
For a metis, attempting to hide one's deformity	0	0	-3
For a lupus, using too many human tools and other Weaver things	0	0	-1/use
Pack:			
Gaining the position of pack leader	0	3	0
Living alone, without one's pack, except for ritual reasons	0	0	-3
Sept and Tribe:			
Performing regular duties and chores for the sept (gained at monthly Moot Rite)	0	1	0
Failing to performing regular duties and chores for the sept (subtracted at monthly Moot Rite)	0	0	-3
Disobeying a caern officer (Caern Warder, etc.) without good reason	0	-1 to -3	0
Serving in any sept position (Caern Warder, etc)	1/year	3/year	1/year
Refusing any sept position (Caern Warder, etc)	-1	-2	-1
Loyal service to a sept	1/year	2/year	1/year
Loyal service to a tribe	1/year	3/year	1/year
Litany:			
Upholding the Litany (depending on the lengths to which a Garou goes)	0	1 to 5	1 to 3
Breaking the Litany (depends on severity of the transgression)	0	-5 to -8	-2 to -4
Challenges:			
Participating in a just challenge	1	2	0
Participating in an unjust challenge	0	-3	0
Challenging someone too far above or too far below your Rank	0	-3	0
Behavior			
Giving good advice	0	0	2
Giving bad advice	0	0	-2
Mediating a dispute fairly	0	3	0
Mediating a dispute unfairly	0	-4	0
Keeping one's promises	0	2	0
Failing to keep one's promises	0	-3	0
Being truthful	0	2	0
Being truthful in the face of extreme adversity	0	5	0
Being deceptive	0	-3	0
Being deceptive in the face of extreme adversity	0	-1	0
Any time trickery backfires	0	0	-2
Attempting to act outside one's auspice, openly (depends on circumstances	0	-1 to -5	0
Telling a good story at a moot	1	0	2
Telling a true epic at a moot that is later retold by others	2	1	3
Telling an epic that is entered into the Silver Record	3	4	6

Activity	Glory	Honor	Wisdom
Speaking dishonorably to one's elders (depends on the severity)	0	-1 to -5	0
Speaking without permission at a moot	0	-1	0
Speaking poorly of the Garou as a whole	0	-2	0
Speaking poorly of one's auspice	0	-4	0
Speaking poorly of one's tribe	0	-4	0
Speaking poorly of one's pack	0	-6	0
Speaking poorly of another tribe (depends on circumstance; doesn't include speaking ill of Bone Gnawers)	0	-1	0
"Crying Wolf" (i.e., summoning the Ahroun of a sept when there is no real danger present)	0	-5	0
Protection and Defense:			
Healing a fellow Garou (non-pack member) unselfishly	0	0	1
Showing mercy to a wayward Garou	0	0	3
Protecting a helpless Garou	0	4	0
Not protecting a helpless Garou	0	-5	0
Protecting a helpless human	0	2	0
Not protecting a helpless human	0	-1	0
Protecting a helpless wolf	0	5	0
Not protecting a helpless wolf	0	-6	0
Supporting an innocent being accused of a crime (who is later proven innocent)	0	5	0
Supporting an innocent being accused of a crime (who is later proven guilty)	0	-4	0
Death while defending your pack	4	6	0
Death in defense of Gaia	7	7	0
Frenzy:			
Succumbing to a berserk frenzy	0	0	-1
Succumbing to a fox frenzy	-1	0	-1
Succumbing to a fox frenzy and abandoning your pack in time of need	0	-1	-2
Succumbing to a berserk frenzy and injuring fellow Garou	0	0	-3
Succumbing to the thrall of the Wyrm	0	0	-4
Performing a heinous act while in the thrall of the Wyrm (cannibalism, perversion, attacking own packmates, etc)	0	-6	0

Human and Kinfolk Relations

Activity	Glory	Honor	Wisdom
Maintaining good relations with nearby Kinfolk	0	0	2
Having poor relations with nearby Kinfolk	0	0	-3
Choosing a mate and breeding	0	0	3
Choosing a mate, but not breeding	0	0	-1
Honorably mated	0	2/year	0
Protecting the Veil	0	4	0
Harming/rending the Veil	0	-5	0
Repairing the Veil (covering up an instance that could reveal the Garou to humans)	0	3	1

Renown Conversion

Of all the changes **Werewolf: The Apocalypse** has undergone between editions, the most dramatic change has probably been the Renown system. In First Edition, Renown wasn't measured in temporary or permanent dots; instead, it was an ever-increasing series of numbers. The higher you got, the higher your Rank.

What does this have to do with the Revised Edition? Not a lot — but there are still a number of first edition books in specialty stores and reprint compilations that use the original Renown system. Many of these books are still quite good, to boot, and contain totems and fetishes found nowhere else. So to use the material in these old books to full effect (and why not?), a Storyteller should be prepared to convert them to Revised rules. Which is where these guidelines come in.

Generally speaking, old Renown awards tended to range from 100 to 2000. (To put this in perspective, characters began the game with a total of 10,000 Renown to qualify them for Rank One, and needed 20,000 to get to Rank Two, 40,000 to get to Rank Three, and so on.) Besting a minor Wyrmish threat would earn 100 Glory, completing an Umbral quest might earn 500 Wisdom, and so on.

The current system recommends Renown awards ranging from one to seven points of temporary Renown, with one point marking a noteworthy but not spectacular deed and seven points being awarded only to those who have made the greatest sacrifices and achieved the greatest deeds.

With that in mind, the simplest thing to do is to convert a Renown award based on that scale. For example, if a book mentions a Renown award of 100-500, that's roughly the equivalent of one or two points of Renown. The following chart denotes our recommended guidelines for Renown conversion; feel free to modify and interpret the results as you like.

Old Renown Award	New Renown Award
100-300	One point
350-750	Two points
800-1200	Three points
1250-1750	Four points
1800-2000	Five points
2001+	Six or seven points

Characters, of course, are something of a different story; there's no good formula for converting their old Renown scores to the modern system. In such a case, Storytellers are encouraged to guesstimate a character's Renown as appropriate for his or her rank or deeds; total accuracy isn't *that* necessary. (Besides, time has certainly passed since the publication of those books, and some of those characters may well have earned an extra rank by now….)

Underwater Combat

Werewolves are far from at their best in the water, but that doesn't mean that they can always choose to fight on dry land. It's entirely possible that a werewolf may be tossed overboard, or be forced into combat in a river, lake or even swimming pool. This can prove a real problem in more than one way — visibility is heavily impaired, and an air-breather cannot rely on scent to track prey. And, of course, there's the difficulty involved with just moving around.

Athletics is the default factor for determining whether a character can swim or not; unless the Storyteller rules otherwise, presume that anyone with at least one dot in Athletics can swim. When underwater, the character's Athletics (or Swimming, if the Storyteller lets characters purchase Swimming as a Secondary Ability rather than an Athletics specialty) governs just how easily she's able to move. A character performing any physical action cannot use more dots in the relevant Ability than she has in Athletics; a werewolf with Melee 5 but Athletics 2 can only use two dots of her Melee Skill when submerged.

Athletics	Base Speed	Sprint Speed
0	1 meter/turn	1 meter/turn
1	1 meter/turn	(Strength +2) meters/turn
2	1 meter/turn	(Strength +4) meters/turn
3	(Strength/2) meters/turn	(Strength +6) meters/turn
4	(Strength/2) meters/turn	(Strength +9) meters/turn
5	(Strength) meters/turn	(Strength +12) meters/turn

Swimming rate is largely determined by training, not agility; water is sufficiently dense that the ability to pull oneself forward is more reliant on strength than speed. The accompanying chart is a good guideline for how quickly a character will be able to move in the water. (If the Storyteller allows Swimming to be purchased as a Secondary Ability, use the chart as if the character possessed an Athletics rating two higher than her Swimming rating.)

When actually embroiled in hand-to-hand combat underwater, a character is at a severe disadvantage. All brawling attacks save grapples and bites halve the attacker's Strength for purposes of damage, and are dodged at –1 difficulty thanks to the slowing effect of the water. Melee weapons are similarly impaired — flexible weapons such as chains and thrown weapons are ineffectual, blunt weapons lose three dice from their damage pools, slashing weapons lose two dice and stabbing weapons lose one.

Firearms are also a risky proposition. Firing on a submerged target from dry land suffers a +2 difficulty to the attack roll, and a bullet loses 1 die of damage for every meter of water it passes through. Firing underwater does not suffer the same difficulty modifier (which is the result of image displacement), but damage is reduced as usual.

As mentioned in the main rules, combat underwater tends to be very stressful, and uses up oxygen much more quickly. During combat, a character can hold his breath for a number of turns equal to twice his Stamina — after that, he begins to drown, taking one health level of lethal damage each turn, which can't be regenerated until he's breathing air once more.

For the definitive look at underwater combat, have a look at **World of Darkness: Blood-Dimmed Tides**.

Weapons

Werewolves don't have to use weapons to be effective in combat, but many prefer not to have to rely on claws and fangs alone. Although firearms are certainly effective, they're a bit *too* easy for most werewolves — learning to use the sword that your ancestors wielded requires discipline, whereas any human can use a firearm. (And, of course, there's the stigma of relying too much on the Weaver's pet advances….) So although most werewolves see no need to use anything other than their natural weaponry, some have a definite taste for melee weapons.

This expanded weapon section is intended to offer Storytellers a much greater variety of weapons with which to confound players — or to offer their characters as fetishes or other heirlooms. Many of these weapons can be found in "silvered" version. These might be crafted entirely from silver — this makes them more useful against werecreatures, but does one less die of damage due to the metal's general inferior edge and hardness (save for klaives, which undergo a special forging process and ritual hardening to achieve their remarkable tensile strength). A weapon might also be silver-plated, in which case it is treated as a silver weapon for maybe one or two blows against a strong target before the silver is worn away. Silver that has been worked into an alloy is irritating and painful, but soakable — it may turn bashing damage into lethal as far as an allergic shapeshifter is concerned, but is unlikely to have much more effect.

• **Axe:** This category includes everything from the size of a fire axe on up; these statistics can be used for Norse battleaxes, a woodcutter's axe, and so on. Axes are fairly popular among Garou, who often fight creatures that need to be bodily hacked to bits before they stop moving (like the undead).

• **Chain:** Although a simple length of chain makes a fine weapon without any alterations, some Eastern cultures attach weights to either end to maximize the chain's hitting power and entangling capability. (In Japan, such a weighted chain is called a manriki-gusari.) It's an easy thing to attach a blade to the end of a chain as well. A character armed with such a combination weapon (such as a kusari-gama, which boasts a weight on one end and a small sickle-like blade on the other) may choose to attack with the blade or the chain on any given action, using the statistics for the knife or chain as appropriate. Werewolves rarely craft chains into fetishes; a werewolf is generally likely to use a chain only as a weapon of opportunity.

• **Club:** The simplest of weapons, this represents any makeshift bludgeon. A club can be a tree branch, a lead pipe, a baseball bat or any such thing. These statistics can also represent the more finely crafted war clubs of many cultures. Werecreatures aren't prone to fabricate fetish clubs; most spirits wouldn't care to enter and empower a simple length of wood. Any club fetishes in existence are probably war clubs appropriate to the people that crafted them.

• **Katana**: The epitome of Japanese weaponsmithing (some would say of the world's weaponsmithing), the katana is a curved sword designed for slashing. It is folded many, many times in the forging process, making a true katana a remarkably fine weapon — unfortunately, buyers are far more likely to run into shoddy knock-offs. The statistics listed are for the finest katanas to be found (which are almost never for sale); lesser blades do one less die of damage. Werewolves do not bind spirits into katanas, and so no fetish katanas can be found outside the Beast Courts. Mundane katanas, however, are popular among some Glass Walkers who enjoy the craftsmanship required to forge such a blade. The exacting forging process of the katana makes it impossible to silver; unless a fetish weapon, a katana will do nothing more dramatic than lethal damage to a werewolf.

• **Knife:** Next to the club, the knife is the most basic weapon there is. These statistics represent short-bladed stabbing or slashing weapons of all sorts: bowie knives, daggers, jambiyas, stilettos, Japanese tantos, and so on. There are a variety of fetish knives, though none so famous (or infamous) as the fang dagger.

• **Labrys**: A preferred weapon of the Black Fury tribe, the labrys is a dangerous double-bladed axe. The Furies commonly make these axes into fetishes, usually granting great speed in combat and howling like banshees when wielded against male foes.

• **Mace:** The mace is the next step up from the club — a hafted weapon with a forged or cast-iron head. A mace can be flanged or spiked (the latter version is often called a morningstar), or simply a smooth metal weight. Designed to stave in skulls and do severe tissue damage, flanged maces are usually considered lethal damage (although at the Storyteller's option, some targets — such as vampires or Crinos-form werebeasts — might be resilient enough to treat a flanged mace's damage as bashing).

• **Polearm:** These weapons were generally the choice of peasantry — at its most basic, a polearm is simply a utensil such as a sickle or cleaver attached to a pole for extra reach. However, more sophisticated versions can be found; these statistics should work well for anything from halberds (a spear combined with a small axe head) to nine-dragon tridents (elaborate Chinese polearms). Fetish polearms are almost unheard of; a Crinos werebeast has plenty of reach, and

Melee Weapons Chart

Weapon	Difficulty	Damage/Type	Conceal
Sap	4	Strength/B	P
Chain	5*	Strength/B	J
Club	5	Strength +1/B	T
Staff	6	Strength+1/B	N
Knife	4	Strength/L	P
Spear	6	Strength +1/L	N
Mace	6	Strength+2/L	N
Sword	6	Strength +2/L	T
Katana	6	Strength +3/L	T
Axe	7	Strength +3/L	N
Polearm	7	Strength+3/L	N
Klaive**	6	Strength +2/A	J
Labrys	7	Strength +3/A***	N
Grand Klaive**	7	Strength +3/A	T

Difficulty: The normal difficulty at which the weapon is used.

Damage: The number of damage dice rolled for the weapon.

Type: B = Bashing; L = Lethal; A = Aggravated

Conceal: P = Pocket; J = Jacket; T = Trenchcoat; N = weapon can't be concealed

*A chain may be used to entangle an opponent's limb at +1 difficulty.

**These weapons are silver and inflict unsoakable damage to Garou.

***Damage code applies only to fetish versions; a labrys without a spirit bound within inflicts lethal damage.

a polearm offers little else to someone whose claws are more deadly than a steel blade.

• **Spear:** Although even a long, sharpened stake can qualify as a spear (Storytellers may want to penalize such crude weapons a die of damage), most spears range from five to fifteen feet in length, with a stone or metal head at one end. They are fairly popular among werebeasts, as the long haft works well in a wielder's hands no matter how large he can grow. Some sample spears include javelins, tridents, flint-tipped spears and boar-spears (which feature crossguards to keep the boars — or enemies — from forcing their way down the shaft to attack the wielder). The short-hafted assegai, notable for its unusually large leaf-shaped head, is a popular weapon among African shapeshifters (usually Bastet). Wendigo are fond of binding spirits of the winds or storms into spears to craft fetishes that manipulate weather or call down ice or lightning.

• **Staff:** This is the standard length of wood or metal, roughly as long as its wielder is tall. A properly wielded staff can be used to great defensive effect; Storytellers may choose to add one to the difficulty to strike (not shoot) a person who has the Melee specialty of staff use and who forgoes attacking in favor of defense for the turn. The Children of Gaia are most likely to create fetish staves, as they appreciate the weapon's utility as a non-lethal weapon.

• **Sword:** These statistics can be used for everything from basket-hilted claymores to Viking broadswords; the differences between them aren't tremendously significant. Generally speaking, the "sword" category covers everything with a blade of about three feet or so — longer than the short sword, shorter than swords that must be used two-handed. Swords are rarely made into fetishes — the grand klaive is of similar size, and much more useful — but some Shadow Lords and Silver Fangs appreciate their symbolic impact.

A Brief History

Although it's very hard to pinpoint specific dates that were important to Garou history — werewolves are creatures of oral tradition, and don't necessarily count years the way that humans do — Storytellers might find a brief outline of Garou history helpful. The following is by no means comprehensive, but it should help give a sense of which event followed which over the millennia.

It may seem that a disproportionate amount of significant events are piling up in the last century — that perception is very true. The Apocalypse is at hand, and each new event that shakes up the war is another one of the signs that the end is near.

Werewolf Timeline

Prehistory

(Although the Garou have many legends of the First Days, many events took place long before humans or werewolves started counting the years. No actual dates exist for most of the prehistoric exploits of the werewolf tribes, but the following prehistoric events are generally — not always — presumed to have happened in the rough order given.)

• Humanity emerges

• Birth of the first Garou

• Impergium begins

• The Wendigo, Croatan and Uktena follow their Kin across the land bridge from Siberia to North America

• The Garou sever and scatter the Talons of the Wyrm, powerful manifestations of the Wyrm in the physical world

• Impergium ends; the first human cities begin to develop

• The War of Rage rages across Europe and parts of Asia and North Africa

General History

1200 BC (approximate) — The Fianna fight the Fomori Wars for possession of the British Isles

1800 BC (approximate) — The Silent Striders are driven from Egypt by the curse of a powerful servant of the Wyrm.

200 (approximate) — The White Howlers fall to the Wyrm; those that don't become Black Spiral Dancers are slain by their corrupted brethren.

600 (approximate) — A massive Umbral fire heralds the beginning of the Dark Ages.

1521 — The death scream of the last werebat echoes across the Penumbra of the Americas; the Shadow Lords renounce war against the Fera of South America.

1589 — The Croatan sacrifice themselves to banish Eater-of-Souls from the physical world.

1780s — Steam engines make the first true factories possible, marking the beginning of the Industrial Revolution.

1796 — Laurent de Mer forms the occult Enlightened Society of the Weeping Moon, a cult founded on garbled interpretations of Black Spiral Dancer lore.

1830s — A powerful Bane is released from its bonds in the American West; it fuses with a similarly mighty Weaver-spirit to become the spiritual menace known as the Storm Eater. Roughly at the same time, the Warder tribe adopts the name "Iron Riders" in sept after sept.

1850s — Vampires begin migrating into the American West in numbers. Human population begins to explode in the West.

1865 — Jeremiah Lassater and his partners incorporate into Premium Oil.

1890 — Thirteen mighty Garou, one from each tribe save the Bunyip, sacrifice themselves in the Rite of Still Skies to seal the Storm Eater once more.

1892 — Jeremiah Lassater makes an unholy pact with a mighty Wyrm-beast, granting it control of Premium Oil through him.

1895 — The Iron Riders elders begin referring to themselves at moots as the "Glass Walkers."

1913 — The last few members of the Enlightened Society of the Weeping Moon disband.

1915 — Premium Oil undergoes a change of management — and a name change to Pentex Incorporated.

1930s — The European Garou of Australia, tricked by the Black Spiral Dancers, exterminate the Bunyip in the War of Tears.

1986 — Pentex moves into Brazil, beginning operations to cull the rainforest for all they can get from it. Werewolves from around the world respond, igniting the War of the Amazon.

1989 — The *Exxon Valdez* disaster, coupled with the Chernobyl disaster of 1986, is cited as proof that the Third Sign of the Prophecy of the Phoenix has come to pass.

1990 — The ancient hag Baba Yaga awakens in Russia.

1992 — Baba Yaga erects the "Shadow Curtain," a powerful Umbral barrier that closes off Russia from the rest of the world (at least spiritually speaking).

1998 — The Russian Garou slay the Zmei Gregornous; concurrently, Baba Yaga is destroyed by persons unknown. The Shadow Curtain crashes down, reuniting the Russian Garou with the rest of the Garou Nation.

1999 — The Red Star, Anthelios, appears in the Umbral skies. A cub is born to two metis parents; the birth is heralded as one of the final signs of Apocalypse. King Albrecht leads a crusade against the Seventh Generation, crushing its leadership. The Beast Courts propose alliance with the Stargazers.

2000 — The Stargazers formally secede from the Garou Nation. The Garou elders admit that the Sixth Sign of the Prophecy of the Phoenix has come to pass, and that the Seventh is surely nigh.

Name:	Breed:	Pack Name:
Player:	Auspice:	Pack Totem:
Chronicle:	Tribe:	Concept:

Attributes

Physical		Social		Mental	
Strength	●OOOO	Charisma	●OOOO	Perception	●OOOO
Dexterity	●OOOO	Manipulation	●OOOO	Intelligence	●OOOO
Stamina	●OOOO	Appearance	●OOOO	Wits	●OOOO

Abilities

Talents		Skills		Knowledges	
Alertness	OOOOO	Animal Ken	OOOOO	Computer	OOOOO
Athletics	OOOOO	Crafts	OOOOO	Enigmas	OOOOO
Brawl	OOOOO	Drive	OOOOO	Investigation	OOOOO
Dodge	OOOOO	Etiquette	OOOOO	Law	OOOOO
Empathy	OOOOO	Firearms	OOOOO	Linguistics	OOOOO
Expression	OOOOO	Leadership	OOOOO	Medicine	OOOOO
Intimidation	OOOOO	Melee	OOOOO	Occult	OOOOO
Primal-Urge	OOOOO	Performance	OOOOO	Politics	OOOOO
Streetwise	OOOOO	Stealth	OOOOO	Rituals	OOOOO
Subterfuge	OOOOO	Survival	OOOOO	Science	OOOOO

Advantages

Backgrounds		Gifts	Gifts
	OOOOO		
	OOOOO		
	OOOOO		
	OOOOO		
	OOOOO		

Renown

Glory

O O O O O O O O O O

❏ ❏ ❏ ❏ ❏ ❏ ❏ ❏ ❏ ❏

Honor

O O O O O O O O O O

❏ ❏ ❏ ❏ ❏ ❏ ❏ ❏ ❏ ❏

Wisdom

O O O O O O O O O O

❏ ❏ ❏ ❏ ❏ ❏ ❏ ❏ ❏ ❏

Rank

Rage

O O O O O O O O O O

❏ ❏ ❏ ❏ ❏ ❏ ❏ ❏ ❏ ❏

Gnosis

O O O O O O O O O O

❏ ❏ ❏ ❏ ❏ ❏ ❏ ❏ ❏ ❏

Willpower

O O O O O O O O O O

❏ ❏ ❏ ❏ ❏ ❏ ❏ ❏ ❏ ❏

Health

Bruised		❏
Hurt	-1	❏
Injured	-1	❏
Wounded	-2	❏
Mauled	-2	❏
Crippled	-5	❏
Incapacitated		❏

Experience

Homid	Glabro	Crinos	Hispo	Lupus
No Change	Strength (+2)____	Strength (+4)____	Strength (+3)____	Strength (+1)____
	Stamina (+2)____	Dexterity (+1)____	Dexterity (+2)____	Dexterity (+2)____
	Appearance (-1)____	Stamina (+3)____	Stamina (+3)____	Stamina (+2)____
	Manipulation (-1)____	Appearance **0**	Manipulation (-3)____	Manipulation (-3)____
		Manipulation (-3)____		
Difficulty: **6**	Difficulty: **7**	Difficulty: **6**	Difficulty: **7**	Difficulty: **6**
		INCITE DELIRIUM IN HUMANS		

Other Traits

____________________OOOOO
____________________OOOOO
____________________OOOOO
____________________OOOOO
____________________OOOOO
____________________OOOOO
____________________OOOOO
____________________OOOOO
____________________OOOOO
____________________OOOOO
____________________OOOOO
____________________OOOOO
____________________OOOOO
____________________OOOOO
____________________OOOOO
____________________OOOOO
____________________OOOOO
____________________OOOOO

Fetishes

Item:____________________ Level____ Gnosis____
Power:____________________
Item:____________________ Level____ Gnosis____
Power:____________________
Item:____________________ Level____ Gnosis____
Power:____________________
Item:____________________ Level____ Gnosis____
Power:____________________

Rites

____
____
____
____
____
____
____
____
____
____

Combat

Maneuver/Weapon	Roll	Difficulty	Damage	Range	Rate	Clip

Brawling Chart

Maneuver	Roll	Diff	Damage
Bite	Dex+Brawl	5	Strength+1/A
Body Tackle	Dex+Brawl	7	Special/B
Claw	Dex+Brawl	6	Strength+1/A
Grapple	Dex+Brawl	6	Strength/B
Kick	Dex+Brawl	7	Strength+1/B
Punch	Dex+Brawl	6	Strength/B

A=Aggravated Damage
B=Bashing Damage

*Armor:*____________________

Nature: **Demeanor:**

Merits & Flaws

Merit	Type	Cost	Flaw	Type	Bonus

Expanded Background

Allies

Mentor

Ancestors

Pure Breed

Contacts

Resources

Kinfolk

Totem

Possessions

Gear (Carried):

Equipment (Owned):

Sept

Name:

Caern Location:

Level: Type:

Totem:

Leader:

Experience

TOTAL:

Gained From:

TOTAL SPENT:

Spent On:

Werewolf: The Apocalypse™

History

Prelude

Description

Age:
Hair:
Eyes:
Race:
Nationality:
Sex:

	Height	Weight
Homid:		
Glabro:		
Crinos:		
Hispo:		
Lupus:		

Battle Scars:

Metis Deformity:

Visuals

Pack Chart

Character Sketch